CALCULATING AND COMPUTING FOR SOCIAL SCIENCE AND ARTS STUDENTS

CALCULATING AND COMPUTING FOR SOCIAL SCIENCE AND ARTS STUDENTS

AN INTRODUCTORY GUIDE

Robert Solomon
Christopher Winch

Open University Press
Celtic Court
22 Ballmoor
Buckingham
MK18 1XW

and
1900 Frost Road, Suite 101
Bristol, PA 19007, USA

First Published 1994

A catalogue record of this book is available from the British Library

ISBN 0 335 19232 7 (pk)   0 335 19233 5 (hk)

Library of Congress Cataloging-in-Publication Data

Solomon, Robert, 1947–
    Calculating and computing for social science and arts students :
an introductory guide / Robert Solomon, Christopher Winch.
        p. cm.
    Includes index.
    ISBN 0–335–19233–5   ISBN 0–335–19232–7 (pbk.)
    1. Mathematics.   2. Computer science.   I. Winch, Christopher.
II. Title.
QA39.2.S65   1994
005.36—dc20   94–16904
                                                            CIP

Typeset by Vision Typesetting, Manchester
Printed in Great Britain by St Edmundsbury Press, Bury St Edmunds, Suffolk

Contents

Acknowledgements

We are very grateful to the following friends, colleagues and relations, who read all or part of the manuscript and made very valuable comments and suggestions: Liz Dawtrey, Gordon Hughes, Adrian Little, Tal Rubinstein, Keith Sharp, Ichiko Shirasu, Katharine Solomon, Jeremy Wilson, Cathy Winch and Michael Wyness. Thanks are due to Jim Perkins and Tracey Sherwood for their help with the photography. Our thanks also to the following for permission to include photographs of their products: Locomotive Software, Packard Bell UK Ltd, Microsoft Ltd and Wordstar International Ltd.

Introduction

If it were ever true that there exists a fixed boundary between the social sciences/arts subjects and the sciences, that boundary is being crossed with increasing frequency. More and more, students in the arts and the social sciences are expected to know how to use computers and to understand some aspects of maths, particularly, although not exclusively, in the area of statistics. We are particularly interested in reaching those of you who are following degrees in which maths and computing do play a role, if not yet a vital one. We aim to give you a summary of the mathematical techniques that you will be likely to come across in your degree course and to give you some idea of what modern computers can do and how they can work for you. We also recognize that both maths and computing will play a part in your life outside the study and the library and we have, therefore, also tried to illustrate how they affect such matters as personal finance and leisure activities.

Why do we think that it is worthwhile your paying attention to maths and computing, even if you are studying a subject like history or politics? Let's take maths first. There is a tendency in the arts and social sciences to make increasing use of mathematical techniques, and particularly statistical techniques, in the interpretation and analysis of information. In part, this is a reaction against what some perceive as a cavalier approach to the collection, interpretation and analysis of data which characterized some of the work carried out in the social sciences in the last twenty or thirty years. It is also a recognition of the fact that mathematics can be an extremely elegant and powerful way of presenting and analysing large amounts of information. Last, but not least, it is also a reflection of the fact that the advent of the microcomputer has made the application of mathematical techniques to data relatively simple and rapid to carry out, even for those who are not professional mathematicians. All these factors have led to a situation where today's undergraduates can no longer ignore maths and computing as irrelevant to their studies. They will in fact benefit from having some knowledge and skill in maths and computing.

We recognize that most students will neither want an advanced text nor one that is too specialized. There are plenty of such books about in both the maths and the computing areas and we have no wish to add to their number. Our own research suggested to us that a simple, fairly general book would satisfy the needs of the greatest number of students and would also give them the opportunity for more advanced and specialized study if that is what they wished to pursue. So we aimed to write a book that is detailed enough to give you some ability to take advantage of maths and computing techniques in your work and everyday life, but which will not be so detailed as to prove daunting to the non-specialist reader.

Calculating and Computing has been written in two parts. Part One deals with the mathematics and statistics that you will need, and Part Two deals with computers and their applications. We have not tried to be exhaustive but to focus on the areas that will be of most use to you. The maths is covered first because we recognize that you will not be able properly to appreciate some of the computer applications without an acquaintance with the mathematical methods that they use. We have used the term 'mathematics' quite widely to include the interpretation of data and the logic of statistical inference as well as more familiar topics like arithmetic and algebra. This has been done so as to revise areas that you will have covered at school and to introduce you to those areas that are likely to be of most use in your work and daily life. The computing subjects that we have covered have been chosen both to introduce you to the basic workings of computers and to those applications that are likely to be of most relevance.

The first chapters deal with arithmetic and algebra and then the book moves on to the interpretation of data, statistical inference and the use of statistical tests. The topics covered form a progression in that each chapter builds on knowledge and skills covered in previous chapters. This does not, however, mean that you have to read Part One from beginning to end if you do not feel that every chapter is relevant to your needs. For example, if you feel very confident about arithmetic, you may move straight on to Chapter 3 on 'Algebra'. You may, however, wish to read the three chapters that are concerned with statistics as a whole.

The first two chapters of Part Two form an introduction to the basic ideas of computing. The ones that follow are more or less self-contained chapters on computing applications. Word-processing, spreadsheets, databases and statistical packages are the ones that you will find most directly relevant both in your studies and in everyday life, and we have concentrated on these. There are many other computing applications, such as accounting and design packages, but these can be followed up in more specialist publications.

The book can be read from cover to cover and there are many readers who will want to tackle it in this way. You can also be selective, looking at one part only or perhaps dipping into chapters. You may also wish to refer to particular sections like, for example, the glossary of computer jargon or the different kinds of statistical tests that are discussed in Chapter 6. Each chapter contains plenty of examples and exercises, which we have designed so that they will be of particular relevance to arts and social sciences students. The exercises are there to deepen your understanding of the topics dealt with in each chapter, but it is not absolutely necessary to do them if you do not wish to do so.

We hope that you will find, as a result of reading the book, that some knowledge of mathematics and computing will enhance your studies and prove to be of use in your everyday life. If it does, then we will feel that we have succeeded in what we set out to do.

PART ONE
Calculating

1   Arithmetic 1

The title of this first chapter is modest. Arithmetic, after all, is studied by children throughout their schooling. Familiarity with the types of numbers, such as whole numbers, negative numbers, fractions and decimals and with the four basic operations of adding, subtracting, multiplying and dividing are necessary for living a successful life in the modern world.

Most people can handle basic arithmetic without any difficulties. If this applies to you, then you probably need to do no more than glance through this chapter to assure yourself that it is all familiar before moving on to the next chapter. But there are many highly educated and intelligent people who find arithmetic disproportionately hard, and whose normally acute minds seize up at the sight of a number or an algebraic symbol. There are also those who take a perverse pleasure in their inability to do arithmetic – it is easy to spot the pride in the claim made by Lord Randolph Churchill, when confronted with decimals, that he 'could never make out what those damn dots meant'.

So if you are one of those people who do find difficulty with arithmetic, even if you never admit to it, this chapter is for you. We hope it is not too patronizing. We have thought it better to explain the obvious than to risk not explaining the obscure.

THE FOUR OPERATIONS

These operations are addition, subtraction, multiplication and division. There are four words to describe the results of the operations:

● When we add two numbers we obtain their *sum*.

The sum of 3 and 2 is 5.

● When we subtract one number from another we obtain their *difference*.

The difference of 8 and 2 is 6.

● When we multiply two numbers we obtain their *product*.

The product of 7 and 3 is 21.

- When we divide one number by another we obtain their *quotient*.

The quotient on dividing 10 by 2 is 5.

If you are sometimes a bit shaky on which of the operations you should use, it might be a good idea to remember for yourself some standard examples of each of the four operations. The examples are all to do with money, as this is the everyday use of arithmetic which people are least likely to get wrong.

- **Adding:** If I buy a beer costing 85p and a packet of crisps for 17p, the total cost is 102p.
- **Subtracting:** The cost of a jacket is £35. If a £5 discount is offered, then the price will be £30.
- **Multiplying:** If I buy a round of 5 beers at 85p each the total cost is 425p.
- **Dividing:**. If a legacy of £2000 is shared equally between 5 people, each will receive £400.

Use of calculator

All the tedium that used to attend the working out of long calculations is now largely a thing of the past. With a calculator it is possible to do the most complicated calculation very quickly. It is still necessary though to be able to use the calculator with confidence and reliability. If you press the wrong buttons, you cannot expect the answer to be correct.

With most calculators presently available, you press in the numbers and the operation in the same order as it is written. After this, you press '=' to obtain the actual result of the calculation. To find $3 + 5$, you press the following:

$$\boxed{3} \; \boxed{+} \; \boxed{5} \; \boxed{=}$$

The answer 8 appears.

Not much can go wrong with this use of a calculator. The following exercises provide practice in the use of a calculator to perform the four basic operations.

Exercises

(a) Find the total profits of Frizle-em Electrical Goods over two years:

Year	Profit
1993	£2,300,004
1994	£ 500,985
Total	_____

(b) An army of 100,000 men sustains 15,000 dead or wounded after a major battle. Calculate the number of able-bodied soldiers remaining.

(c) A social security benefits office pays out £278,000 each week. Assuming payments continue at the same level, how much does it pay out each month? How much does it pay out each year?

(d) 3000 children score below 80 on a numeracy test. In order to boost their performances, so that they all achieve a score of at least 100, each child will need an average of 19 hours tuition time. How many teacher hours will be needed in order to give the children effective help? Assuming that tuition costs £15 an hour, how much will the total programme cost?

(e) The wage bill for a bus company's drivers is £2,400,000. Given that all 200 drivers are on the same rate of pay, what is the basic wage of each driver?

(f) An EU grant for infrastructural works is presented to the government of Ruritania. The total for this grant is 114,000,000 ecus. It is a condition of receiving it that the Ruritanian government shares the grant equally among all six provinces of the country. How many ecus does each province receive?

(g) A tax rebate of £20,400 has to be shared equally among 150 taxpayers. How much money will each taxpayer get?

FRACTIONS

The word fraction comes from the same source as *fracture*. It means that a whole number is broken into parts. If 1 is broken into two equal parts they are halves, if into three equal parts they are thirds, and so on.

These are the simplest sort of fractions, with 1 on the top, such as $\frac{1}{4}$ or $\frac{1}{7}$. We can multiply these simple fractions, to get three-quarters ($\frac{3}{4}$), or four-sevenths ($\frac{4}{7}$) and so on. If the fraction is greater than 1, then we have a vulgar or improper fraction, such as $\frac{8}{7}$ or $\frac{11}{4}$. These vulgar fractions can be converted to mixed numbers, which have a whole number part and a fractional part:

$$\frac{8}{7} = 1\frac{1}{7} \qquad \frac{11}{4} = 2\frac{3}{4}$$

Fractions and mixed numbers abounded in pre-decimal currency. Each pound was divided into 20 shillings, and each shilling into 12 pence. Each penny was divided into 2 halfpennies, or 4 farthings. So a sum of money could be $9\frac{3}{4}$d (ninepence three farthings) and so on. In order not to be out of pocket, people were all expert with the basic arithmetic of fractions.

Adding and subtracting

We cannot add two fractions by simply adding the tops and the bottoms. The sum of $\frac{1}{2}$ and $\frac{1}{4}$ is not $\frac{2}{6}$. Before adding or subtracting, we must ensure that they are the same sort of fractions, that is, they have the same number on the bottom (called the *denominator*). For the example above, to add $\frac{1}{2}$ and $\frac{1}{4}$ we first convert the half to quarters:

$$\frac{1}{2} = \frac{2}{4} \qquad \text{A half equals two quarters.}$$

Now we can add, as both fractions are expressed in terms of quarters:

$$\tfrac{1}{2} + \tfrac{1}{4} = \tfrac{2}{4} + \tfrac{1}{4} = \tfrac{3}{4}$$

In the days of pre-decimal currency, this operation was trivial. People were well aware that the sum of a halfpenny and a farthing was three farthings.

The example above is about the simplest we can get. But the principle applies to more complicated sums. To add or subtract two fractions, you must ensure that the denominators are the same. This can be done by multiplying the tops and bottoms of the fractions.

Suppose we need to add $\tfrac{2}{5}$ and $\tfrac{3}{7}$. We need to ensure that the denominators of the fractions are the same. Multiply the top and bottom of the first fraction by 7, and multiply the top and bottom of the second fraction by 5. Then both fractions will have the same denominator of 35:

$$\tfrac{2}{5} + \tfrac{3}{7} = \tfrac{14}{35} + \tfrac{15}{35} = \tfrac{29}{35}$$

Exercises   (a) $\tfrac{1}{10}$ of all students studying agriculture get first-class degrees and $\tfrac{3}{10}$ get a 2:1. What fraction of all the agriculture students gain a degree of 2:1 or higher?

(b) $\tfrac{7}{100}$ of the male population of Ruritania have had some homosexual experience. $\tfrac{1}{100}$ are exclusively homosexual. What fraction are bisexual?

(c) $\tfrac{2}{5}$ of the patients in a hospital are over 65, and $\tfrac{1}{3}$ are under 5. What fraction are either over 65 or under 5?

(d) $\tfrac{1}{6}$ of the students at Lowlands University are studying a natural science subject. $\tfrac{1}{10}$ of the students study physics. What fraction of the students study a science other than physics?

Multiplication

The multiplication of fractions is easier than addition and subtraction. You multiply the tops and multiply the bottoms. For example, suppose $\tfrac{4}{7}$ of students attending a college are female, and of these $\tfrac{1}{5}$ live at home. The fraction of students attending the college who are female and who live at home is:

$$\tfrac{4}{7} \times \tfrac{1}{5} = \tfrac{4}{35}$$

One particular case is when we multiply a fraction by a whole number. We multiply the top by this whole number, but not the bottom:

$$4 \times \tfrac{3}{4} = \tfrac{12}{4} = 3$$

(We can think of 4 as $\frac{4}{1}$, and then apply the rule above.) Notice that here the result is no longer a fraction. In general, if a fraction is multiplied by its denominator, the result is a whole number.

Division

Division of fractions is reasonably straightforward. To divide by a fraction, you turn it upside down and then multiply:

$$\tfrac{2}{7} \div \tfrac{3}{4} = \tfrac{2}{7} \times \tfrac{4}{3} = \tfrac{8}{21}$$

A special case occurs when we divide a whole number by a fraction. The result will be larger than the original number:

$$7 \div \tfrac{1}{4} = 7 \times \tfrac{4}{1} = 28$$

An interpretation of this calculation in terms of old money is as follows. How many farthings are there in 7 pence? The answer is $7 \times 4 = 28$, as there are 4 farthings in each of the 7 pennies.

Exercises
(a) An army field hospital has 2 litres of a painkiller. Each dose consists of $\frac{1}{125}$ of a litre. How many doses are there?
(b) $\frac{49}{100}$ of the population of Ruritania are male, and of them $\frac{2}{5}$ live below the poverty line. What fraction of the total population of Ruritania are men below the poverty line?
(c) $\frac{1}{30}$ of the population of a city are drug addicts. Of these $\frac{2}{3}$ are HIV-positive. What fraction of the city population are HIV-positive drug addicts?

Use of calculator
If you have a scientific calculator, it will be able to work directly in fractions. There will be a button labelled $\boxed{\text{a b/c}}$, or similar. To enter a fraction you press this button in between the top and the bottom. To enter $\frac{3}{7}$, you press:

$$\boxed{3} \quad \boxed{\text{a b/c}} \quad \boxed{7}$$

Now ordinary arithmetic can be done.

You can also enter mixed numbers, like $2\frac{3}{5}$. You press the $\boxed{\text{a b/c}}$ button twice, in the following sequence:

$$\boxed{2} \quad \boxed{\text{a b/c}} \quad \boxed{3} \quad \boxed{\text{a b/c}} \quad \boxed{5}$$

With a bit of practice you can become confident at the arithmetic of fractions with the use of a calculator. You can check your answers to the problems of this section with a calculator.

DECIMALS

Decimal notation provides another way of writing parts of whole numbers. The digit immediately after the decimal point gives the number of tenths, the second digit gives the number of hundredths, and so on. So, for example:

$$2.35 = 2 + \tfrac{3}{10} + \tfrac{5}{100}$$

This is immediately understandable in terms of decimal currency. A bill of £2.35 can be paid for by two £1 coins, three 10p pieces, and five 1p pieces.

Use of calculator

To enter a number involving decimals, you make use of the button labelled $\boxed{.}$. To enter 2.35, the sequence is:

$$\boxed{2}\ \boxed{.}\boxed{3}\ \boxed{5}$$

Now ordinary arithmetic can be done.

PERCENTAGES, RATIOS, PROPORTIONS

Fractions of one sort or another occur so frequently throughout all forms of study that there are several ways of expressing them. Percentages, ratios and proportions can all be thought of as ways of dealing with fractions.

Percentages

A percentage is a fraction in which the denominator is always 100. So 15% is the same as $\tfrac{15}{100}$. It is particularly easy to convert between decimals and percentages, as one just moves the decimal point two places to the left or to the right:

$$15\% = 0.15$$

The advantage of expressing things in percentages is that the fractional nature is disguised for those who might be frightened by it.

Some things are *always* expressed in terms of percentages. For example:

● *Interest rates*: A bank interest rate (the interest charged on loans) might be 9%.
● *VAT rates*: At the time of writing, the VAT rate is $17\tfrac{1}{2}$%.

Some things are *sometimes* expressed in terms of percentages. For example:

● *Income tax*: Sometimes we say that the tax rate is 25%, sometimes we say it is 25p in the £.

● *Pass rates*: We could either say that the pass rate for the driving test is 40%, or that 40 people out of a 100 pass.

Ratios

To compare two numbers, we often do so by means of a ratio. This is very like expressing one of the numbers as a fraction of the other. For example, suppose we have a recipe for vinaigrette, requiring 4 spoonfuls of oil and 1 spoonful of vinegar. We could describe the vinaigrette by saying that:

The ratio of oil to vinegar is 4:1

This ratio will still hold if we make larger quantities of the vinaigrette. We could make double the quantity with 8 spoonfuls of oil and 2 of vinegar, or if making a catering size quantity, 12 pints of oil for 3 pints of vinegar. In all cases the ratio is the same:

$$12:3 = 8:2 = 4:1$$

We can convert the ratio to a fraction by expressing the amount of vinegar as a fraction of the amount of oil. In all the cases, the amount of vinegar is a quarter that of the oil:

$$\tfrac{3}{12} = \tfrac{2}{8} = \tfrac{1}{4}$$

Exercises

(a) The ratio of officers to all ranks in a division of 20,000 men is 1:40. How many officers are there? What is the percentage of officers in the division?

(b) The ratio of first-class honours degrees to all degrees in a university is 1:30. How many first-class degrees will there be in a graduation cohort of 6000? What percentage of the cohort obtains first-class degrees?

(c) In a city, the ratio of car owners to non-car owners is 2:3. If there are 400,000 car owners, how many non-car owners are there? What is the total population of the city?

Increase in ratio

In many circumstances, we can express an increase in terms of the ratio of the amount before to the amount after. Suppose that the workforce of a factory has increased in the ratio 4:5. That means that for every 4 workers employed before, 5 are employed now. We have divided the number of workers by 4 and multiplied the result by 5. So the number of workers employed has been multiplied by $\tfrac{5}{4}$. For example, if there were 2000 workers before, the number after will be $2000 \times \tfrac{5}{4} = 2500$. This is obtained by dividing 2000 by 4 to get 500, and then multiplying this by 5 to get 2500.

Exercises   (a) A salary bill has increased in the past year in the ratio 6:7. If last year's bill was £600,000, what is this year's bill?

(b) A city's crime rate has increased in the ratio 5:6 since last year. If there were 2500 crimes last year, how many were there this year?

(c) The number of people literate in a country has increased in the ratio 8:9 over the last ten years. 15,350,000 were literate ten years ago. How many are literate today?

Division in ratio

Suppose something is built up out of two components. It might be the vinaigrette, which contains both oil and vinegar. The amounts of each component can be given by a ratio. For this example, we say that vinaigrette contains oil and vinegar in the ratio 4:1.

Suppose we have 20 ounces of this vinaigrette. How much of each component does it contain? As it contains them in the ratio 4:1, it can be divided into 5 equal parts, of which 4 are oil and 1 vinegar. So by use of fractions we can find the quantities of each.

$$\text{amount of oil} = \tfrac{4}{5} \times 20 = 16 \text{ oz}$$
$$\text{amount of vinegar} = \tfrac{1}{5} \times 20 = 4 \text{ oz}$$

The use of ratios can be extended beyond fractions. Something may contain more than two constituent parts, and we can still show the sizes of these parts by a ratio. Suppose that the votes in a constituency are divided between Conservative, Labour, Liberal Democrats in the ratio 5:4:3. This ratio summarizes several fractions: that the Labour vote is $\tfrac{4}{5}$ of the Conservative, that the Liberal Democrat vote is $\tfrac{3}{4}$ of the Labour, that the Liberal Democrat vote is $\tfrac{3}{5}$ of the Conservative.

Suppose that the total number of votes was 60,000. These are divided in the ratio 5:4:3, so the total is divided into $5 + 4 + 3 = 12$ equal shares. So the number of Conservative votes is:

$$\tfrac{5}{12} \times 60,000 = 25,000 \text{ votes.}$$

Exercises   (a) A survey of the use of public libraries finds that the ratio of users to non-users is 2:3. If the population of a town is 200,000, how many use the public library?

(b) A psychologist uses a test to classify people as either divergent or convergent thinkers. The ratio of these two groups is 3:8. In a group of 1001 people, how many are convergent thinkers?

(c) In the election example above, how many people voted Labour and how many Liberal Democratic?

Proportions

Proportion is another way to describe fractional parts. Suppose we have a class of 20 students, of whom 9 are female. We could say that the proportion of women is 9 in 20. Notice that there are many other ways we can express the proportion:

- The percentage of women is 45%
- Women make up $\frac{9}{20}$ of the class
- Women make up 0.45 of the class
- The ratio of women to men is 9:11.

Exercises
(a) The proportion of vegetarians in the student body of a university is 1 in 5. If there are 10,000 students in the university, how many are vegetarian?
(b) The proportion of members of ethnic minorities in a constituency is 2 in 7. If the constituency contains 105,000 people, how many come from ethnic minorities?

NEGATIVE NUMBERS

Here we enter one of the traditionally difficult areas of arithmetic: What do negative numbers mean? Why do we need them? Why do they obey the rules they do? These are common questions that are often not answered satisfactorily.

What do they mean?

In a way, they mean what we choose to make them mean. But they occur in contexts like the following. Suppose we have a scale, which extends upwards from 0, 1, 2, and so on. If that scale also extends downwards, then we use negative numbers to describe the downwards values.

Examples
- *Temperature*: We can have a temperature of $-10°$.
- *Bank balances*: If you have an overdraft of £50, your account stands at $-£50$.
- *Trade balances*: If there is a trade deficit of £100,000,000, the balance is $-£100,000,000$.
- *Height above sea level*: The Dead Sea is 400 m *below* sea level, so its height *above* sea level is $-400\,$m.

Why do we need them?

In a way, we don't absolutely need them. Science and mathematics developed perfectly happily for thousands of years without them. Any statement involving negative numbers can be rephrased so that we only use positive numbers. For example:

- Instead of a temperature of $-50°$, we can speak of $50°$ below zero.
- Instead of a trade surplus of $-£300,000,000$, we can speak of a trade deficit of $+£300,000,000$.

There is nothing wrong with this. It means though that we will have to do more writing. To take the temperature example, there is a formula which converts Celsius temperature to Fahrenheit:

$$F = 32 + \tfrac{9}{5}C$$

If we allow C to be negative, then this formula works for all values of C. If we restrict ourselves to positive numbers only, then we will have to use at least two formulas:

$$F = 32 + \tfrac{9}{5}C \text{ if C is above zero}$$
$$F = 32 - \tfrac{9}{5}C \text{ if C is below zero}$$

Why do they obey the rules they do?

> Minus times minus equals a plus,
> The reason for this we need not discuss.

This rhyme stems from the exasperation of teachers unable to give an explanation for the rule: 'minus times minus = plus'. Essentially, they are falling back on: 'It's true because I say so'. It is extraordinarily difficult to give a satisfactory explanation for the rule, other than that it works. One justification is as follows:

Suppose that at your bank you have an overdraft of £50. This means that your account stands at $-£50$. Suppose also that your bank manager, in a sudden fit of generosity, cancels your overdraft. This is as if he has *subtracted* your overdraft, so essentially he has given you a present of £50:

$$-(-£50) = +£50$$

Exercises   (a) A local authority School Psychological Service wishes to administer a general aptitude test to the 11-year-olds in the area and then convert the scores into a score for Mental Age. The test has a 100 items and each correct item is scored 1 and each incorrect item is scored -1. Billy gets 40 right and 60 wrong. Ruchera gets 55 right and 45 wrong. What are their scores? What is the difference between their scores?

(b) The Edwards family bought a house for £100,000. Two years later its value had fallen to £70,000. What is the value of the house to them, given that a mortgage of £80,000 is still outstanding? (This is called *negative equity*.)

Use of calculator

For most calculators, when you enter a negative number, you do not press the ⊟ button. Instead, you enter a positive number, and then press the ± button. The sequence to verify the 'minus times minus' rule is:

This enters -3 times -5. The answer should be $+15$.

Use your calculator to verify the answers to some of the exercises in this section.

CASE STUDY: COSTS OF EDUCATION

What follows is a business example of the economics connected with an independent school. The figures are real. You will be asked to work out various results for expenses to parents and useful calculations for the school itself.

Table 1.1 gives the annual cost of educating a child at a private school, broken down into items of expenditure. Alongside each amount is a figure giving its percentage of the total bill. For example, the annual cost of teachers' salaries for a boarding pupil is £2845, which is 41% of the bill as a whole.

Table 1.1   The annual cost of educating a child at a private school

	Boarding pupil		Day pupil	
	£	%	£	%
Wages and salaries				
Teachers	2845	41	2190	58.3
Other staff	959	14	390	10.4
Catering	841	12	330	9
Books, teaching materials, games,				
entertainment	455	6.5	135	3.6
Property				
Rates, insurance, fuel, lighting	488	7	129	3
Repair and maintenance to property				
and ground	1011	14.5	397	11
General expenses	357	5	184	5
Total	6956		3755	

Source: Macintyre and Co.

Exercises   (a) Darren Scott is a boarder and Jeremy Scott is a day boy. What is the total school fee bill for the Scotts?

(b) How much cheaper is Jeremy to educate than Darren?

(c) The school has 62 boarders and 325 day pupils. What is the total fee income?

(d) An old boy donates an annual sum of £35,000 to the school to provide bursaries for the offspring of poor single parents. How many boarders will the money support? How many day pupils will the money support?

(e) What proportion of a boarding school's expenses go on salaries for all staff? What is the ratio of teachers' salaries to other salaries?

(f) What is the percentage difference between what a boarding school pays on catering and what a day school pays on catering?

(g) What is the ratio of boarders to day pupils in (c)?

(h) If the number of boarders increases to 100, what is the ratio now of day boys to boarders?

(i) The costs of running the school are £350,000, regardless of how many pupils there are. If there are only 12 boarders and 50 day pupils, by how much is the school 'in the red' for one year? What is the minimum number of extra boarders required to make the school 'break even'? What is the minimum number of extra day pupils required to make the school 'break even'?

(j) Suppose that the school is co-educational, and there are the same numbers of day pupils and boarders as in (c). $\frac{1}{5}$th of the day pupils are girls. What is the ratio of girl day pupils to pupils as a whole?

2   Arithmetic 2: Many operations

Chapter 1 dealt, essentially, with single arithmetical operations. You may have skipped that chapter, if you felt that you were able to handle these operations with confidence. However, when we have more than one operation to do, things become more complicated. Even highly numerate people are liable to make mistakes when evaluating a complicated formula.

Once again, please forgive us if in the following sections we seem to be stating the obvious.

ORDER OF OPERATIONS

Suppose we are about to perform more than one arithmetical operation. First let us deal with two cases which do not pose much difficulty.

Several additions

If we have several numbers to add together, it doesn't matter what order we use. The answer will always be the same:

$$2 + 3 + 5 = 3 + 5 + 2 = 5 + 3 + 2, \text{etc.}$$

If you have bought a lot of items at the supermarket, then when their prices are added up at the checkout, it doesn't matter which items come first and which last. You will end up paying the same amount of money regardless.

Several multiplications

If we have several numbers to multiply together, it doesn't matter what order we use. The answer will always be the same.

$$2 \times 3 \times 5 = 3 \times 5 \times 2 = 5 \times 3 \times 2, \text{etc.}$$

If we are working out the volume of a fridge which is 20 cm deep, 30 cm wide and 50 cm high, then we can multiply these numbers in any order. The volume of the fridge will not depend on whether we take the height or the width or the length first.

Use of calculator

All calculators, even the simplest, will deal correctly with successive additions or multiplications. After all, many people have bought calculators to help with the sort of situations described above, of adding up a list of prices, or evaluating the volume of a fridge.

Addition and multiplication

Now the situation does become more complicated. If we apply both addition and multiplication to numbers, it does matter which order the operations are done in. Suppose we are taking:

12 plus 15 times 5

Do we do the plus first or the times? If we do the plus first, we get:

12 plus 15 = 27
27 times 5 = 135

If we do the times first, we get:

15 times 5 = 75
12 plus 75 = 87

We have deliberately written the problem using the words 'plus' and 'times'. Written in symbols it becomes:

$$12 + 15 \times 5$$

With an expression of this sort, the rule is that the multiplication is done before the addition. So the second interpretation is the correct one.

An interpretation of the problem above is as follows. Suppose a plumber charges a call-out fee of £12, and then charges for his labour at £15 per hour. How much will you have to pay if he does 5 hours work? You will have to pay the £12 charge, and then 5 lots of £15. The total bill will be:

$$£12 + £15 \times 5$$

When working this out, you do the multiplication first to find the labour charge, and then add on the call-out charge. You do not add the £12 and the £15, and then multiply by 5. There is a direct interpretation of this mistake: it is as if the plumber were including the call-out charge, not just once for the visit, but for every hour he was working.

Use of calculator

When we have multiplication and addition in the same problem, the rule is to do the multiplication first. If you have a scientific calculator, it has been programmed to obey this rule. So when you key in the sum:

the correct answer of £87 will appear.

But if you have a simple, non-scientific calculator, it may not function correctly. Keying in the above may give a result of 135. So be aware of the limitations of your calculator, and if necessary break down the calculation into two steps. Do the multiplication first, then the addition.

Exercises

(a) For the final assessment of a course, the coursework marks are halved and then the exam mark is added. What is the final assessment for a student who got 226 in coursework and 87 in the exam?

(b) A money changer will change £ to $ at a rate of $1.5 per £1. He will then charge a commission of $10. How many dollars will you get for £160?

(c) A writer's income consists of £5000 on which tax at 25% has been paid, and £22,000 on which tax has not been paid. What is the total income after tax has been paid on all the income?

BRACKETS

Mathematical notation and scientific calculators both have the rule of doing the multiplication before the addition. But what if we want to do the addition first? The following is an example.

Mr and Mrs Smith go on holiday to France, Mr Smith taking £120 of spending money and Mrs Smith £160. How much French money will they have in total, at a rate of 9 French francs to the £? If they pool their British money, they will have $120 + 160 = 280$. Converting this to FF gives $280 \times 9 = 2520$ FF. In terms of symbols this is:

$$120 + 160 = 280$$
$$280 \times 9 = 2520$$

If we write the calculation in one line, we get:

$$120 + 160 \times 9$$

By the rule we have so far, of doing the multiplication first, the result would be $120 + 1440 = 1560$. This is incorrect, and furthermore it is nonsense in terms of the original situation. It is as if we have converted Mrs Smith's pounds to francs, and then added on Mr Smith's pounds without converting them.

To show that we want to do the addition before the multiplication, we put it in *brackets*. The expression is:

$$(120 + 160) \times 9$$

The brackets give priority to any operation. The operation inside must be done first, before any operation outside. The correct use of brackets is one of the topics that causes the greatest difficulties in school education – when mathematics teachers are opened up at a post-mortem, they are often found to have the word 'brackets' engraved upon their hearts.

Use of calculator

If you have a scientific calculator, then it will be able to use brackets. For the expression above, key it in as it is written.

You can have layers of brackets, nested within each other. On many scientific calculators you can have up to six layers.

Expansion

If you don't have a scientific calculator, or if for some reason you want to work out an expression without using brackets, then there is an operation called *expansion* to get rid of them. In the example above, we can expand the brackets by multiplying both terms by 9:

$$(120 + 160) \times 9 = 120 \times 9 + 160 \times 9$$

This rule can be justified in terms of the example above as follows. The left-hand side is what happens if Mr and Mrs Smith pool their British money and take it along to the bureau de change to convert it into French francs. Suppose instead that they are no longer on speaking terms after the first day of the holiday. Mr Smith will take his £120 and change it to 120×9 FF, and Mrs Smith will convert her £160 to 160×9 FF separately. The total amount they receive is the sum of these, the right-hand side of the expression above. Obviously, the two sums of money are equal.

BODMAS

So far we have only mentioned addition and multiplication. The other operations are subtraction and division. Another symbol occurs when we have one expression over another, as in:

$$\frac{2 + 3}{4 + 7}$$

Putting one expression over another is rather like putting the expressions in brackets. The additions on top and bottom must be done before the division. So the fraction above is equal to $\frac{5}{11}$. We could obtain the same result by writing it as:

$$(2 + 3) \div (4 + 7)$$

So now, on top of the four operations of addition, subtraction, multiplication and division, we have the procedures of putting expressions in brackets or over each other. The 'word' BODMAS gives the order of priority for the operations:

Brackets Over Division Multiplication Addition Subtraction

Exercises

(a) A dose of medicine consists of 1 ml painkiller and 4 ml anti-clotting agent. How much medicine is required for 48 patients?

(b) The manufacturers of Frizle-em electric toasters have recalled the August batch from customers because of a fault which leads to the customer rather than the slice of bread being scorched. In order to forestall legal action, they offer each customer a £200 voucher for Frizle-em electrical products, together with a new toaster. Work out the total cost of the operation for the firm given that 2000 toasters were sold in August, and that each costs £56.

(c) In a village of 300 there are 90 men who can read and 70 women who can read. What is the proportion of readers in the village?

(d) The population of Ruritania is divided into Christian and non-Christian. The north-eastern province of Ruritania has 2 cities with adult populations over 500,000. Here are the figures for each city, together with figures for females and non-Christian males:

	Total population	Females	Non-Christian males
City 1	708,953	412,765	12,063
City 2	669,140	456,142	8,087

(i)   Find the male Christian population in each city.
(ii) Find the total male Christian population of both cities.
(iii) If all 11 provinces have the same number of male Christians in cities over 500,000 as the north-eastern province, then what is the total?

(e) Intelligence Quotient (IQ) is arrived at in the following way. Add all the scores on items on an intelligence test and divide by the number of items. This gives the subject's mental age. The mental age is then divided by the subject's chronological age. The result is then multiplied by 100 to arrive at a standard figure irrespective of age.

Alison scores as follows on 5 items on a certain scale:

Item 1   11
Item 2   18
Item 3   17
Item 4   13
Item 5   11

(i)   Find Alison's total score. What is her mental age?
(ii) Alison is 10 years old. What is her IQ according to this scale?
(f)   Ron and five friends go to a restaurant. The total bill for drinks comes to £36. Ron suggests that they divide it equally. What will the bill be for each of the party?

Ayesha, however, objects that she has not drank any wine, only 1 bottle of Vesuvius mineral water at £1.50. If the other 5 people drank wine, calculate how much each should pay towards the drinks bill.

The total cost of the meal comes to £150. Ron and his friends produce three vouchers, each worth £15 to offset the cost. What total do they have to pay after presenting the vouchers?

ACCURACY AND ROUNDING

Suppose that in a sociological or educational context you have the following: In a city of 2,000,000 people, $\frac{1}{7}$ of the population are between 10 and 15. How many children of that age range are there?

The arithmetic is straightforward. Put 2,000,000 into your calculator, and divide by 7. The answer on a 10 figure calculator is:

$$285714.2857$$

One cannot have 0.2857 of a 10- to 15-year-old, so we could take the whole number part of the answer. One would then say that the number of children in this age range is 285,714. This answer is also unsatisfactory. It is given very accurately – it implies that there are exactly this number of children, not 285,713 or 285,715.

It would be impossible to count the number of children so accurately. For a start, during the counting process, many children would be moving in or out of the age range. It also assumes that we can define exactly who is a resident of the city and who a temporary visitor, and exactly where the boundaries of the city are. So it is misleading to give the answer as an exact number of children.

Notice another thing. The population of the city was given as 2,000,000. It is very unlikely that there are exactly two million people in the city. The figure of two million is only an approximation – it could vary by many thousands on either side of it. And if the given population could be out by many thousand, one cannot predict accurately the number of children. One cannot deduce accurate results from inaccurate information.

In the circumstances, the answer we obtain should indicate that we have only a rough idea of the number of children in the age range. Probably, it would be best to say that the number of children is 300,000. What we have done is to *round* the answer obtained from a calculator. We have rounded it to the nearest 100,000; that is, the answer of 285,714 is nearer 300,000 than 200,000.

Exercises   (a) The total trade deficit for a 3 month period is £92,200,000. Assuming that the deficit is the same in each month, find the monthly deficit, rounding the answer to an appropriate value. At this rate, what would be the annual deficit? Round the answer to an appropriate value.
(b) Recall that IQ is defined as mental age divided by chronological age, multiplied by 100. Ellen is aged 11, and has a mental age of 12. What is her IQ? Round your answer to an appropriate value. Alan, age 8, has an IQ of 87. What is his mental age?

Decimal places

The example above dealt with whole numbers, as you cannot have a fraction of a child. Some quantities like weight, length and time can be measured in fractions and decimals.

Suppose you weigh a parcel on the scales at a Post Office. You find that it weights 1.23 kg. The number 3 is in the second decimal place, and we have measured the weight to an accuracy of two decimal places.

Post Office scales are not very accurate measuring devices – they do not need to be. For parcels they only need to be accurate to two decimal places, as in the example above. If we wanted to find the weight of the parcel more accurately, we could take it to the scales in a physics laboratory, which might have an accuracy of 6 decimal places. We might then find that the parcel weighs 1.232945 kg.

By giving an answer to a certain number of decimal places, we show how accurate the measurement is. Another example concerns time. In the 1928 Olympic Games, the winning time for the men's 100 m was 10.8 seconds. In the 1932 games, it was 10.38. Notice the increase in accuracy – in 1928 ordinary stop-watches were used, and they were accurate only to 1 decimal place. In the next games, automatic timing, capable of an accuracy of 2 decimal places, had been introduced.

Exercises   (a) Overdraft charges are usually given to an accuracy of one decimal place. Here are the charges for different banks expressed as percentages.

Nunnery National	12.5
Caledonian	11.5
Brackleys	7.2
Pughs	7.1
Lowland	7.2
EastProv	9.3

   (i) The figures given represent the annual rate of interest. Divide Nunnery National's rate by 12 to find the *monthly* rate. Round the figure to one decimal place.

   (ii) Find the average annual rate for these banks, by adding and dividing by 6. Round your answer to 2 decimal places.

(b) When exam marks are calculated, they are often in decimals. They are usually rounded up to whole numbers. For example, here are a student's marks in the different papers of a music exam: history 67%, theory 56%, composition 52%, practice 78%. Work out her total mark, then divide by 4 and round to the nearest whole number to find her final mark.

   (i) What are this music student's results expressed to the nearest whole number?

   (ii) Suppose the total of her marks had been 219. What would her final rounded mark be?

(c) The average number of children per family in a country is 2.467. How many children would there be in 212 families? Round your answer to the nearest 10 children.

Significant figures

Suppose a weight is given in kilograms to an accuracy of 2 decimal places, as for the parcel above. This is an absolute measure of accuracy. It says that the weight cannot be more than 0.01 kg from the one given.

This degree of accuracy may not be appropriate for other objects. We could not hope to measure the weight of an ocean liner, for example, to this degree of accuracy. It would not be appropriate for small objects. If we had a small quantity of medicine, say only a few grams, then its weight to the nearest 0.01 kg would be 0.00 kg. This would not be very helpful when dispensing the medicine! We need a much greater degree of accuracy.

So there is often a need for a *relative* measure of accuracy, one that will take account of how large or small the thing being measured is. This is done by expressing a measurement to a certain number of significant figures. Take the number 52.034. The leftmost digit, the 5, is the first significant figure. The 2 is the second significant figure, and the 0 the third. The whole number has been expressed to 5 significant figures.

If the number given is less than 1, the significant figures start from the first non-zero digit. We do not count the zeros as significant. So for the number 0.0503, the first significant figure is 5, the second is 0, the third 3. The whole number is expressed to 3 significant figures. Because we only start counting significant figures at the first non-zero digit, this measure of accuracy takes account of how large or small the number is. The following measurements are all to 3 significant figures:

$$\text{Weight of ocean liner} = 54{,}300{,}000\,\text{kg}$$
$$\text{Weight of parcel} = 1.34\,\text{kg}$$
$$\text{Weight of measure of medicine} = 0.00134\,\text{kg}$$

Exercises
(a) The population of Ruritania is 36,789,126. Express this to 3 significant figures.
(b) A country's population is divided into ethnic groupings as follows.

Whites	5,000,000
Blacks	30,000,000
Coloureds	8,000,000

Work out the fraction of coloureds in the total population and express the result to 2 significant figures. Do the same thing for the other 2 ethnic groupings.
(c) £1267 is converted to Deutschmarks at a rate of DM2.43 per £. What is the amount in Deutschmarks, expressed to two significant figures?
(d) In 1979, the annual accident rate was 1.05 per head of the population. In ten years, this increased by 58%. What was the annual accident rate per head in 1989, expressed to three significant figures?

POWERS

There is another operation on numbers on top of the four basic ones. This is taking *powers*, or exponentiation. Very often we have to multiply a number by itself. This is called *squaring* the number. (Because when we find the area of a square, we multiply the side by itself.) Instead of writing 5×5, we write 5^2.

If we multiply by the number again, the result is the *cube* of the number. (Because when we find the volume of a cube, we multiply the three sides together.) Instead of writing $5 \times 5 \times 5$, we write 5^3.

And so on. Though there is no physical interpretation of multiplying four lengths together, we can still do so arithmetically. The result is the fourth power, and written 5^4.

Use of   A scientific calculator can work out powers. There is a button labelled x^y,
calculator y^x or a^x. (It depends on the make and the model.) The button sequence for
                    finding 5^4 is:

$$\boxed{5} \ \boxed{x^y} \ \boxed{4} \ \boxed{=}$$

The answer 625 should appear.

Square roots

The square of 3 is $3 \times 3 = 9$. If we want to go in the opposite direction, from
9 to 3, we take the *square root*. The square root of 9 is 3. The symbol for
square root is $\sqrt{\ }$. So $\sqrt{9} = 3$.

On a calculator, even on many simple ones, you will find a square root
button. The sequence to find $\sqrt{9}$ is:

$$\boxed{9} \ \boxed{\sqrt{\ }}$$

Note that you do not need to press the $\boxed{=}$ button.

Priority

Taking powers has priority over multiplication and division. So, for example:

$$2 \times 3^2 = 2 \times 9 = 18$$
$$16 \div 2^3 = 16 \div 8 = 2$$

So you do the taking of powers first, and then the multiplication or division.
If you want to do the multiplication or division first, then brackets must be
used. *Brackets take priority over everything*:

$$(2 \times 3)^2 = 6^2 = 36$$
$$(16 \div 2)^3 = 8^3 = 512$$

Multiplying powers

Suppose we have two powers to multiply together. This can be done in a
particularly simple way. Suppose we are multiplying 2^3 and 2^4. Write them
out in full:

$$2^3 \times 2^4 = (2 \times 2 \times 2) \times (2 \times 2 \times 2 \times 2)$$

Here we have seven 2's, multiplied together:

$$2^3 \times 2^4 = 2^7$$

So when we multiply powers of 2, we *add* the powers.

Exercises (a) A room is a perfect cube of side 12 feet. What is the area of the ceiling? What is the volume of the room?

(b) Two measures of the spread of data are the *variance* and the *standard deviation*. The variance is the square of the standard deviation.

(i) If the standard deviation is 23, what is the variance?

(ii) If the variance is 169, what is the standard deviation?

CASE STUDIES

Computer memory

In Part Two we shall be discussing computers. Here is a suitable place to link up the way computer memory is described with some of the work of this chapter.

The basic unit of computer memory is the *byte*. A byte will hold one letter, or one number. Obviously, a computer will use many bytes when running a program. The memory of a computer is described in terms of the number of bytes it can use.

The kilobyte (kB) is approximately 1000 bytes. Kilo comes from the Greek for 1000, as in kilogram or kilometre. In fact, a kilobyte is a bit more than 1000 bytes. Because computers work in binary operations, it is $2^{10} = 1024$ bytes.

The BBC Model A computer has a memory of 16 kB. This is 2^4 kB, so the total number of bytes is $2^4 \times 2^{10} = 2^{14}$ bytes. The Amstrad PCW has a memory of $256 = 2^8$ kB. How many bytes is this, expressed as a power of 2?

The next unit up is the megabyte (MB), which is approximately 1000 kilobytes, i.e. a million bytes. (The Greeks had no word for a million. Mega comes from the Greek for huge.) In fact, it is 2^{10} kB. How many bytes are there in a MB, expressed as a power of 2? A powerful personal computer might have a memory of 16 MB. How many bytes is this, expressed as a power of 2?

Next we have gigabytes (1 gigabyte = 1024 MB). The word is derived from the Greek for giant. After that terabytes (1 terabyte = 1024 gigabytes). Tera comes from the Greek for monster. Express as powers of 2 the number of bytes in a gigabyte and in a terabyte.

Statistical formulas

Later in the book we deal with statistics. Here is an appropriate place to practise our handling of a calculator with statistical formulas.

Mean or average

To find the mean of a set of n numbers, add them up and divide by n. Suppose we want the mean of the five numbers 98, 87, 79, 92, 84. This will be:

$$\frac{98 + 87 + 79 + 92 + 84}{5}$$

There are several ways we could evaluate it using a calculator. We could enter the top line, press ☐ , then divide by 5. Or we could use the equivalent expression for the mean:

$$(98 + 87 + 79 + 92 + 84) \div 5$$

Evaluate this mean, by whichever way you find easiest.

Variance

The variance of a set of numbers is a measure of how widely spread they are. Suppose you have found the mean of the numbers above to be m. Then the variance is:

$$\frac{(98 - m)^2 + (87 - m)^2 + (79 - m)^2 + (92 - m)^2 + (84 - m)^2}{5}$$

Evaluate the variance of the five numbers above.

Personal finance

Exercises   Liz Smith is a student who is a single parent. Her annual income comes from the following various sources:

Grant	£2875
Child allowance	£1411
Maintenance payments	£3264
Rent from lodger	£1040

(a) What is her total annual income?

Her annual fixed costs are as follows:

Mortgage	£720
Heating and lighting	£300
Council tax	£150
Car expenses	£1906
Children's clothes, childcare and food	£2660

(b) What percentage of Ms Smith's income is paid on her mortgage?
(c) What is her weekly mortgage payment to the nearest £?

Liz Smith runs a car, an elderly Amalgamated Motors Turkey. The costs of running this are considerable, and include 'invisible' items like depreciation and unforeseeable ones like breakdowns. The annual running costs of her car include:

Loan repayments	£600
Insurance	£70
Petrol	£520
Depreciation	£260
AA membership	£70
Repairs	£150
Expenses relating to MOT certificate	£80
Parking fines	£36
Road Fund	£120

(d) What is the total annual cost of running 'The Turkey'?

The amount spent per week will vary.

(e) What is the average weekly cost of running the car? Give your answer to an appropriate degree of accuracy.

Although the car is much more expensive than the bus and the occasional taxi, Liz reckons that the convenience it affords is at least equivalent to the extra money spent. Annual fares on public transport and taxis would cost Liz £660 if she did not have the car.

(f) What is the smallest amount that the car is worth to her each month, in terms of convenience over other forms of transport? Express this figure to the nearest £10.

Personal banking

Choosing a bank can be difficult given the bewildering variety of interest rates, overdraft charges and incentives that banks now offer to students. With the information that is available, however, it is possible to calculate which would be the best deal to suit your own circumstances. Some of the major banks and building societies offer students a free overdraft up to a certain limit. Once that limit has been exceeded, they charge overdrafts at a given percentage rate. Table 2.1 gives the extra incentives to new customers, the level of overdraft which is allowed free of interest and the interest rate on overdrafts exceeding the free limit.

Table 2.1 Overdraft charges and incentives

Bank/society	Incentive	Interest-free overdraft	Interest on excess overdraft
Nunnery National			12.5%
Caledonian		£400	11.5%
Brackleys	£10 voucher	£400	7.2%
Blubberhouses B.S.		£300	10.0%
Pughs	£16 railcard	£400	7.1%
Lowland	£25	£400	7.2%
EastProv	£25	£400	9.3%
Londonderry	Phonecard, radio		8.0%
Royal Bank of Lenzie	£10	£400	7.0%

Work out which is the best deal for you. You will have to supply some of the figures yourself, as these will depend on your own habits and preferences. You will also have to estimate the figures as best you can, since only you will know how much you are likely to be overdrawn and how valuable you consider a radio or a railcard to be.

3   Algebra

In the previous two chapters, we dealt with numbers. Algebra can also deal with numbers, but in a more general way. Instead of dealing with a single number at a time, algebra can deal with all possible numbers by using a letter in their place.

The transition between arithmetic and algebra is one that many people have found difficult to make. Though they can perform arithmetic operations on actual numbers, they find it hard to apply the same operations to letters which stand for the numbers. A great amount of practice is often needed before one becomes expert at algebraic calculations, which is why algebra has got a bad reputation as the most dry and repetitive of subjects.

Why do we need to know it? If algebra is so difficult and dispiriting, why do we need to study it in the first place? There are many reasons why algebra is necessary for many subjects to advance beyond the basic level – here are two.

Generality

An expression containing numbers deals with those numbers only. The corresponding algebraic expression deals with all possible numbers.

To take a domestic example, suppose that you have a cooker whose oven temperature is calibrated in Fahrenheit, but that your favourite cookbook gives temperatures in Celsius. Very often you will need to convert temperatures from one scale to the other. One way would be to prepare a chart giving corresponding temperatures, which might look like:

°C	100	125	150	175	200	225	250
°F	212	257	302	347	392	437	482

Note that only a few conversions are given, whereas in theory there are infinitely many possible ones.

The formula which converts Celsius to Fahrenheit is:

$$F = \tfrac{9}{5}C + 32$$

Here C stands for the temperature in Celsius, and F for the corresponding temperature in Fahrenheit. The formula is general, it works for the infinitely many possible cases. It will work for your cooker temperature, for the temperature given in weather reports, for the temperature reported in scientific experiments, and so on.

Brevity

Another advantage of using algebra is that it saves time and space. In the example above, the single algebraic formula covered all the cases (and infinitely more) in the conversion table. In the actual statement of a scientific or sociological result, the use of algebra saves a lot of writing.

Traditional scientific statements were written out in full. Below is Newton's Second Law (translated from Latin):

> Change in momentum is proportional to the impressed force, and acts along the same straight line as that impressed force.

In algebraic symbols this becomes:

$$\mathbf{a} \propto \mathbf{F}$$

which is rather shorter.

So we hope you are convinced of the benefits of algebra to generalize and shorten numerical work. If you still find it difficult, don't worry that you are being exceptionally slow. Difficulties with algebra are very common, indeed almost universal. An indication that the subject is hard is the length of time that it took to be developed. In all the millenia of mathematical activity, it is only in the last few centuries that we have had anything like a useful algebraic notation.

SUBSTITUTION

So in an algebraic expression we have letters standing for the unknown numbers. When we want to use the expression in a particular case, we replace the letters by the numbers for our case. This process is called *substitution*.

Let us continue with our temperature example. We have our formula for converting from Celsius to Fahrenheit. Suppose that a recipe in the cookbook instructs you to set the oven temperature to 200° Celsius. What should you turn the dial on your cooker to?

Substitute the number 200 for the letter C, so that the formula becomes:

$$F = \tfrac{9}{5} \times 200 + 32$$

Now it is a matter of arithmetic.

Multiply 200 by 9, obtaining 1800
Divide 1800 by 5, obtaining 360
Add 32 to 360, obtaining 392

So set the dial on the oven to 392°, and whatever goes wrong with the cooking cannot be blamed on mathematics!

In subjects like economics, sociology or psychology, you may be presented with an algebraic formula, which covers all the cases of a given situation. You have the numbers for a particular case, which you then substitute into the formula. Below are some examples for you to practise on.

Exercises

(a) *Currency conversion*: The rate of conversion of £ into $ is given by $D = 1.52P$, where P is the number of pounds I have and D the number of dollars I will get. How many dollars do I get for £300?

(b) *Administering medicine*: The amount of a certain medicine to be administered depends on the patient's weight. A person of weight k kilograms should receive $0.02k + 1$ millilitres. How much should be given to a patient weighing 70 kg?

(c) *Psychological testing*: The reliability of a test is r. (Reliability is a measure of how consistent the test is, if applied again.) If the test is made longer, by having n times as many questions, the reliability is now:

$$r' = \frac{nr}{1 + (n-1)r}$$

If the reliability was originally 0.5, what will it be if the test is made 3 times as long?

(d) *Production*: A simple model of the production of a particular product might be that when the price is P, the annual production is:

$$Q = 10,000 + 1000P$$

Find how many items are produced if the price is 4.

(e) Another model of production (there are almost as many models of production as there are economists) is the *Cobb–Douglas* model. Let the labour available be L, the capital available be K and the amount Q produced be:

$$Q = L^{\alpha}K^{1-\alpha}$$

(here α is a constant, measuring the relative importance of labour and capital). Find the production if $L = 100,000$, $K = 300,000,000$ and $\alpha = 0.25$.

CONSTRUCTING FORMULAS

In the previous section we dealt with substituting numbers into formulas which were provided for us. These formulas do not come from thin air – someone must have discovered or created them. You will need to know how formulas are constructed, in order to follow the steps in an argument and to amend or even construct formulas of your own.

When constructing an algebraic formula, we are setting up a general rule which will work in infinitely many possible cases. Typically, we will want to find one quantity in terms of others. In the temperature example, the recipe book gives the Celsius temperature, but we want the temperature in Fahrenheit.

So there will be one or more quantities we have to deal with – the time, the weight, price and so on, it depends what field we are working in. We see what arithmetic operations are needed to obtain the required quantity in terms of the given ones. We take letters to stand for these quantities, and then perform these operations, writing down the result as an expression.

If you are stuck about what operations to use or how to write them, one thing to think is: 'What would I do with actual numbers?' This is illustrated in the following example.

How long does a journey of d miles take at a speed of s mph?

Do we multiply or divide? And which way up should it go? If in doubt, think of an actual journey that you might be familiar with.

How long does a journey of 120 miles take at a speed of 40 mph?

If you imagine yourself doing this journey by car, the answer will be immediate: 3 hours. What have you done? You have divided the distance by the speed. As you did it to the numbers, you must do the same to the letters:

A journey of d miles at s mph takes d/s hours.

Note that if you do the wrong thing, multiply instead of divide, or divide the wrong way up, you will get an answer which would be absurd if done to actual numbers. If you multiplied, you would get the journey taking 4800 hours, about 6 months. If you divide the speed by the distance instead of the distance by the speed, you will get a time of $\frac{1}{3}$ hour.

Exercises

(a) *Currency exchange*: The rate of exchange for pounds to French francs is FF8.5 per £. How many FF do I get for £P?

(b) *Intelligence Quotient*: The IQ of a child is defined as its mental age divided by its real age, multiplied by 100. If a child has real age a and mental age m, what is its IQ?

(c) *Another economic model*: Let the amount of money in circulation be M, the velocity of money (the speed with which it changes hands) V, the quantity of goods available Q and the price of goods P. The product of the money supply and its velocity is equal to the product of the quantity of goods and their price. Express this as an equation in M, V, Q and P.

(d) *Personal economics*: My fixed expenses are E and my disposable income I. After paying the fixed expenses I spend 0.8 of what is left over, and save the rest. Find formulas for the amount left over after paying the fixed expenses, and for the amount I save.

ALGEBRAIC MANIPULATION

In many circumstances, we have to do more than create formulas and use them. Expressions have to be changed around and altered, perhaps to show that one formula is equivalent to another, or to rewrite it in a way that is easier to handle. The example of temperature converts Celsius to Fahrenheit: we might be in the opposite situation, of owning a cooker which is marked in Celsius and a recipe book giving temperatures in Fahrenheit. In this case, we would want to do the conversion the other way round, so that we would have a formula which converts Fahrenheit to Celsius. In this case and many others, we will have to manipulate an algebraic expression. What rules and methods are there for doing this?

Adding and subtracting terms

Suppose you have a collection of algebraic terms, added together or subtracted. They might be:

$$5a + 10a + 20b$$

Then we can simplify by adding terms which are the same sort. In the examples above, we can add the a's together, but we cannot add the $20b$ term because it involves a different letter. The simplification is:

$$15a + 20b$$

It might help to think of money. Suppose that on returning from a trip to America you find in your wallet:

a £5 note, a £10 note, a \$20 bill.

The money you have is £15 plus \$20. You cannot combine the pounds and the dollars until you go into a bank to change one of the currencies.

Multiplying and dividing

When algebraic expressions are multiplied together, we do not always need to put in the multiplication sign '×'. The product of *a* and *b* can be written just as *ab*.

$$a \times b = ab$$

(Note that this cannot be done with numbers: we would not know whether 23 meant two times three or twenty-three.)

It doesn't matter in which order the terms occur: *ab* is the same as *ba*. When finding the area of a wall, it doesn't matter whether you multiply the length by the height or the height by the length.

When we multiply an algebraic expression by a number, often we can leave out the multiplication sign: $3 \times a$ can be written as $3a$, as there is no danger of ambiguity arising. By convention, we usually put the number first. It isn't wrong to write *a*3, it just looks rather unusual.

When we multiply an algebraic symbol by itself, the result is its square: *a* multiplied by itself is a^2. It isn't wrong to write it as *aa* or as $a \times a$, but these are less efficient.

Algebraic fractions

You can make ordinary numerical fractions by putting one number over another. Similarly, you can make algebraic fractions by putting one algebraic symbol or symbols over others. The symbols stand for numbers, and the same rules apply.

When you have ordinary fractions with the same denominator, you can add their numerators:

$$\tfrac{3}{7} + \tfrac{2}{7} = \tfrac{5}{7}$$

The same applies to algebraic fractions.

$$\frac{a}{c} + \frac{b}{c} = \frac{a+b}{c}$$

When fractions don't have the same denominator, then we must adjust them before adding or subtracting. In particular, this holds if one of the numbers is a whole number:

$$1 - \frac{a}{b} = \frac{b}{b} - \frac{a}{b} = \frac{b-a}{b}$$

We write the 1 as *b/b*, so that this fraction will have the same denominator as the *a/b*.

Examples   (a) *The statistics of sociology*: The following formula occurs when fitting a straight line to figures.

$$\frac{\text{ESS}}{\text{TSS}} + \frac{\text{RSS}}{\text{TSS}}$$

where ESS stands for expected sum of squares, RSS for residual sum of squares, and TSS for total sum of squares. Show that you can simplify the expression to:

$$\frac{\text{ESS} + \text{RSS}}{\text{TSS}}$$

The following formula occurs in the situation above, of fitting a straight line to figures:

$$1 - \frac{\text{ESS}}{\text{TSS}}$$

Reduce this expression to a single algebraic fraction with the same denominator as the fraction above.

(b) *Consumption and income*: Suppose my income before tax is I. If the tax rate is 25%, what is my disposable income D? My fixed expenses are E. How much is left after paying these expenses, in terms of D and E? How much is left, in terms of I and E?

STRAIGHT LINE EQUATIONS

A very common procedure in many subjects, such as sociology, economics and psychology, is the fitting of a straight line to data. The reason is that a straight line is a very simple shape to draw and to find the equation of.

Suppose we have the straight line shown in Fig. 3.1. There are infinitely many points on it, for example $(0, 1)$, $(1, 3)$, $(2, 5)$ and so on. Notice that in every case the y-value can be obtained by doubling the x-value and adding 1. So the *equation* of this line is:

$$y = 2x + 1$$

The general equation of a straight line is $y = mx + c$, where m and c are constant numbers. The interpretation is as follows: m represents the *gradient* or *slope*. This is the ratio of the y increase to the x increase. c represents the place where the line crosses the y-axis. It is the value of y when x is zero. Here is an example.

A plumber charges a £12 call-out charge, and £15 per hour after that. How much will he charge for x hours' work? For each of the x hours, he

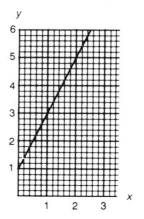

Figure 3.1

will charge £15. So for the time taken, he will charge $15x$. Add on the initial call-out charge:

$$\text{Charge} = 15x + 12$$

Note that the 15 represents the gradient of the corresponding graph. It is the rate per hour, or the increase in charge for each additional hour (see Fig. 3.2). The 12 represents the charge when $x = 0$. It is the amount you have to pay even if no work is done.

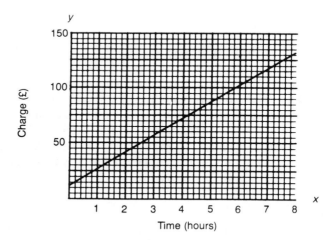

Figure 3.2

Exercises   (a) A psychologist tests the effects of alcohol on agility. A task is performed, and the number of mistakes made after consuming x pints of beer is found to be:

$$\text{Number} = 3x + 5$$

Draw the graph of this function on the diagram in Fig. 3.3.

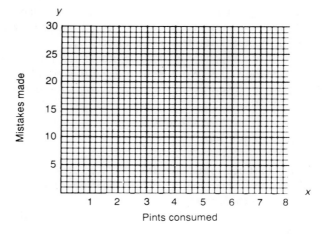

Figure 3.3

Here 3 represents the gradient of the corresponding graph. It gives the number of extra mistakes for each pint of beer consumed. The number 5 represents the number of mistakes made when x is zero, i.e. the number of mistakes made when stone cold sober.

(b) If the price of a commodity is x pounds, then the average consumption of it is given by:

$$\text{average consumption} = 30 - 5x$$

Draw the graph of this function on the diagram in Fig. 3.4.

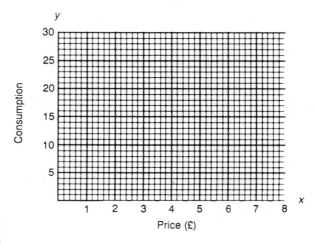

Figure 3.4

Note that here the gradient is negative. The more expensive a thing is the less people buy of it. (Though there are strange commodities, called Giffen Goods, for which the consumption *falls* when the price falls.) Here the negative gradient means that 5 fewer will be consumed for each price rise of £1. The 30 represents the consumption if the price were zero, i.e. the amount people would use if it were absolutely free.

In this case, there is another interesting point – where the straight line crosses the *x*-axis. What is the price at this point? Here consumption is zero, because at this price the item has become too expensive for anyone to buy.

Solving equations

This is a huge topic, comprising a vast area of mathematics. We shall only deal with a very small part of it, the solving of linear equations. These are related to the straight line formulas above.

In each case, to solve an equation is to find the value of the unknown letter. Here is an example:

$$\text{Solve the equation } 12 + 15x = 87$$

The basic rule when solving an equation is: *Do to the left what you do to the right*. The first step is to subtract 12 from both sides, in order to get the $15x$ by itself:

$$15x = 87 - 12 = 75$$

Now we divide both sides by 15, in order to get the *x* by itself.

$$x = \tfrac{75}{15} = 5$$

So our answer is 5. This example connects up with the plumber example above: If the plumber has charged £87, how much work has he done? The answer is 5 hours.

Notice how naturally the algebra of solving this equation connects with the way we would solve the problem by common sense. Of the £87 bill, £12 has gone on the call-out charge, leaving £75. At a rate of £15 per hour, we have got $\tfrac{75}{15} = 5$ hours work done.

Exercises   (a) Solve the equation $3x + 5 = 23$. (Note that this connects with the psychology example above: How many pints of beer must one consume to make 23 mistakes in the agility test?)

(b) Solve the equation $30 - 5x = 20$. (Note how this connects with the economics example above: If the average consumption of the item is 20, what is its cost?)

Changing the subject

Recall that our general straight line equation was $y = mx + c$. Suppose we want to write it so that x is written in terms of the other letters. This procedure is known as *changing the subject*. The steps are the same as for solving the equation when we have numerical values for y, m and c.

Subtract c from both sides:

$$y - c = mx$$

Divide both sides by m:

$$\frac{y - c}{m} = x$$

Now x is the subject of the formula. We can find x directly once we know what the other letters stand for.

Exercises

(a) Make x the subject of the formula: $m = 3x + 5$. (This refers to the example of dexterity above. Find the number of pints consumed from the number of mistakes made.)

(b) Make x the subject of the formula: $C = 30 - 5x$. (This refers to the example of consumption above. Find the price which will give a consumption of C.)

(c) *Economics*: A formula which occurs in economics is $MV = PQ$. Express V in terms of the other letters.

(d) Mental age m, real age a and IQ x are related by $x = 100m/a$. Express m in terms of x and a. Express a in terms of m and x.

(e) *Interval scales*: Suppose, in a statistical context, data are arranged in intervals. Let two intervals be a to b, and b to c. If the intervals are equal, then:

$$b - a = c - b$$

Express c in terms of a and b.

Substitute this expression for c to show that the interval between a and c (which is $c - a$) is twice that between a and b (which is $b - a$).

(f) *Multiple-choice tests*: When you take a multiple-choice test, you answer the questions you know and guess the rest. From your final score, how can the marker find the number of questions you knew the answer of?

Suppose there are T questions, each of which has A possible answers. Suppose you know the answers to R of the questions. Then you will guess the answers to the remaining $T - R$ questions. On average, you will get $1/A$ of these guesses right. So your final score S will be:

$$S = R + 1/A(T - R)$$

Make R the subject of this formula. (Multiply both sides by A, then collect the R terms.)

STATISTICAL FORMULAS

Social scientists are most likely to meet complicated mathematics in the use of statistics. So here we present a section devoted to statistical formulas, in particular to evaluating them. In Chapter 2, we looked at various formulas in terms of numbers. Here we look at the same formulas from an algebraic point of view.

In many statistical formulas, you will see the symbol Σ (Greek capital S, pronounced *sigma*). Now this does not stand for a number, instead it stands for a process on numbers. It means that we add up a whole collection of numbers.

Suppose we have 30 measurements. We could symbolize them as x_1, x_2, x_3 and all the way up to x_{30}. We would often want to add all these measurements up, to find their average for example. It would be tiresome to have to write out every single one of the x_i, and so we use the Σ symbol:

$$\sum_{i=1}^{30} x_i \text{ means the sum } x_1 + x_2 + x_3 + \cdots + x_{30}$$

Mean

Let us start with the mean, which is probably the most easily understood statistical measure. To find the mean of a set of n numbers, add them up and divide by n. Using the Σ symbol:

$$\bar{x} = 1/n \sum_{i=1}^{n} x_i$$

Let us take 6 numbers, $x_1 = 5$, $x_2 = 6$, $x_3 = 4$, $x_4 = 8$, $x_5 = 3$, $x_6 = 7$. The mean of these numbers is given by:

$$\tfrac{1}{6}(5 + 6 + 4 + 8 + 3 + 7) = \tfrac{1}{6} \times 33 = 5.5$$

Variance

The variance of a set of numbers is a measure of how widely dispersed they are. The formula is:

$$\text{var}(x) = 1/n \sum_{i=1}^{n} x_i^2 - x^2$$

In words, the variance is: 'The mean of the squares minus the square of the mean'.

Let us evaluate the variance for the six numbers given above. First add up the squares of the numbers and divide by 6:

$$\frac{1}{6} \sum_{i=1}^{6} x_i^2 = \frac{1}{6}(25 + 36 + 16 + 64 + 9 + 49) = \frac{1}{6} \times 199 = 33.17$$

Now subtract the square of 5.5:

$$\text{the variance is } 33.17 - 5.5^2 = 2.92$$

Correlation

The correlation coefficient between two variables x and y is a measure of how closely they are connected. It is given by the formula:

$$r = \frac{1/n \sum x_i y_i - \bar{x}\bar{y}}{\sqrt{\text{var}(x)} \sqrt{\text{var}(y)}}$$

Let us suppose that the y values corresponding to the x values are:

$$y_1 = 23, \; y_2 = 25, \; y_3 = 26, \; y_4 = 30, \; y_5 = 20, \; y_6 = 28$$

To find $1/n \sum x_i y_i$, multiply the pairs of x and y values, add and then divide by 6. We obtain:

$$(5 \times 23 + 6 \times 25 + 4 \times 26 + 8 \times 30 + 3 \times 20 + 7 \times 28)/6 = 144.17$$

We already know that $\bar{x} = 5.5$ and that $\text{var}(x) = 2.92$. By similar calculations we find that $\bar{y} = 25.33$ and $\text{var}(y) = 10.56$. We have all the components for the correlation coefficient.

$$r = \frac{144.17 - 5.5 \times 25.33}{\sqrt{2.92} \sqrt{10.56}} = 0.871$$

Exercise   (a) Using the figures below, find $\bar{x}$, $\bar{y}$, $\text{var}(x)$, $\text{var}(y)$ and the correlation coefficient r:

x	1	2	3	4	5	6	7	8
y	0.9	1.2	1.5	1.6	2.1	2.8	2.5	3.2

Use of calculator   If you have a fairly sophisticated calculator, it may be able to work out the mean, variance and correlation coefficient of data. Use it to check the results of this section.

CASE STUDIES

We shall end this chapter with a couple of topics which involve algebra.

Substitution rule

In many higher education courses, assessment is done in whole or in part from the results obtained by assignments submitted throughout the year. There is often a scheme to prevent the final result being dragged down by a couple of bad assignments. This is called a *substitution rule*.

Suppose there are 10 assignments throughout the year. The average for all 10 is found. This average is then *substituted* for the two assignments with lowest marks, and a new average calculated. Suppose a student has obtained the following marks for her first 9 assignments:

$$43 \quad 56 \quad 2 \quad 38 \quad 41 \quad 66 \quad 0 \quad 50 \quad 61$$

1. Suppose she fails to submit the 10th assignment. What will be her overall total, after the substitution rule has been applied?

Add up all the marks, then divide by 10. We obtain $357/10 = 35.7$. She got 0 for the 7th and 10th assignments, so replace these scores by 35.7 and recalculate the average. We obtain 42.84.

2. Suppose that the pass-mark for the course is 45. What must she get for the 10th assignment in order to pass?

Suppose she gets a score of x. Then her total for the year will be $357 + x$. The average will be $(357 + x)/10$. Substitute this for the two lowest marks, which are 2 and 0. The new marks are:

$$43 \quad 56 \quad (357 + x)/10 \quad 38 \quad 41 \quad 66 \quad (357 + x)/10 \quad 50 \quad 61 \quad x$$

Add these up, combining the x-terms, to obtain $426.4 + 1.2x$. The new average is $(426.4 + 1.2x)/10$.

If she just passes, this new average is just 45. We obtain the equation:

$$(426.4 + 1.2x)/10 = 45$$
$$426.4 + 1.2x = 450 \quad \text{(multiplying both sides by 10)}$$
$$1.2x = 450 - 426.4 = 23.6 \quad \text{(subtracting 426.4 from both sides)}$$
$$x = 19.7 \quad \text{(dividing both sides by 1.2)}$$

So she must get at least 20 for the last assignment in order to pass.

Exercises   (a) What is the final score for a person whose marks in the 10 assignments were:

$$68 \quad 76 \quad 86 \quad 55 \quad 91 \quad 60 \quad 62 \quad 73 \quad 91 \quad 88 \quad ?$$

(b) Each assignment is marked out of 100. For the first 8 assignments a student obtained:

$$30 \quad 43 \quad 5 \quad 38 \quad 38 \quad 10 \quad 31 \quad 46$$

Can this student achieve a final score of over 45?
(c) What is the least number of assignments a student can submit and still pass?
(d) Show that it is possible for two students to submit the same number of assignments, and gain the same average mark, and yet for one student to pass and the other to fail.

Voting systems

There are very many different voting systems in use. Members of Parliament in the UK and of Congress in the USA are elected by a simple 'first past the post' system. Other more complicated systems have been proposed.

A constituency in the UK returns only one member. The electors cast their votes for a person, rather than for a party. Suppose instead that we have a constituency which returns several members, and for which people vote for the party rather than the candidate. One method is as follows.

Largest remainder

Suppose that there are n seats available, and that T votes have been cast for all the parties combined. Work out $Q = T/(n + 1)$. This is called the *Droop quota*.

Add up the votes received by each party. If an individual party has received v votes, then work out v/Q. Take the whole number part of this expression. The party will receive this number of seats.

Probably not all the seats will be allocated. So see which parties have the largest remainder when v is divided by Q, and allocate the remaining seats to them.

Let us apply this method to an election. Suppose a constituency has 5 seats, and 600,000 people vote. The Droop quota is:

$$600,000/(5 + 1) = 100,000$$

Suppose there are five parties contesting the constituency, and that the results of the election are:

A: 250,000 votes   B: 190,000   C: 50,000   D: 80,000   E: 30,000

On division by Q we obtain:

A: 2.5   B: 1.9   C: 0.5   D: 0.8   E: 0.3

So A immediately gets 2 places and B gets 1. The remainders are 0.5, 0.9, 0.5, 0.8 and 0.3. The largest are 0.9 and 0.8, so the remaining 2 places go to B and D.

Largest divisor

Another system is as follows. There are several rounds of allocation of places. At each stage, if a party with v votes has been allocated r places, we work out $v/(r + 1)$. The party with the greatest value of this expression receives a place, and the expression is recalculated.

Let us take the figures above. Initially, no party has received a place. So $r = 0$ for each party. Work out the expression:

A: $250,000/(0 + 1) = 250,000$ B: $190,000/(0 + 1) = 190,000$
C: $50,000/(0 + 1) = 50,000$ D: $80,000/(0 + 1) = 80,000$
E: $30,000/(0 + 1) = 30,000$

The largest value is for party A, which then receives a place. For A, r is now 1. For the other parties, r is still 0. Recalculate the averages:

A: $250,000/(1 + 1) = 125,000$ B: $190,000/(0 + 1) = 190,000$
C: $50,000/(0 + 1) = 50,000$ D: $80,000/(0 + 1) = 80,000$
E: $30,000/(0 + 1) = 30,000$

The largest value is now for B, which then receives a place. The process can be continued until all the places have been allocated.

Exercises

(a) Finish off the process above, until all 5 seats have been allocated. Is the result the same as for the previous method?
(b) A constituency has 6 seats, contested by 4 parties. What is the result of the following voting, under each of the two systems?

A: 120,000   B: 60,000   C: 90,000   D: 80,000

4   Interpreting data

After a statistical survey or investigation, there is usually a great mass of data to be made sense of. It is very difficult to look at a page full of numbers and draw any useful conclusions. The facts have to be organized in some way before we can base any judgement or action upon them.

TABLES AND GRAPHS

Tables and graphs are economical ways of representing a great number of facts. It is up to the readers of the table or graph to select the information that they need. There are techniques to do this which are not at all difficult to master. Even if you are confronted by a great mass of figures, the important thing is not to panic but to look slowly and deliberately at the table or graph so that you understand the kind of information that it is intended to convey. When you have done this, you will be in a position to ask the questions that you want answered. You will be able to pick out the information you want, either particular items or general trends.

Tables

In a table, information is classified under two headings. You might be interested in the relationship between the income and age of the employees of a company. The information is put into rows and columns: each row might refer to a given age range, and each column to a given level of income. The table might look like that in Table 4.1.

By finding where a row and a column meet each other, you can gain a piece of information such as the number of people in their forties who earn between £30,000 and £40,000. The 30–40 column meets the 40–50 row at the place shaded, and we see that there are 45 people in this category.

The entries in a table do not have to be numerical. Table 4.2 is a straightforward example of a table, which shows the different interest rates offered on credit cards by different banks. Notice that the rows are set out

Table 4.1   Employees by income and age

Age (years)	Income (£000's)				
	0–10	*10–20*	*20–30*	*30–40*	*40+*
16–20	23	34	2	0	0
20–30	57	187	156	24	6
30–40	31	213	191	44	23
40–50	12	154	241	45	18
50–60	2	48	92	61	25

Table 4.2   Highest and lowest interest rates offered on credit cards (22 August 1993)

Card	%
Lowest rates	
1 Robert Fleming/ Save and Prosper (Visa)	14.6
2 Bank of Cyprus (Visa)	19.6
3 National and Provincial (Visa)	21.6
4 Barclays (Mastercard)	21.6
5 First Direct (Visa)	22.2
Highest rates	
33 Bank of Ireland (NI) (Visa/Mastercard)	26.4
34 Bank of Ireland (GB) (Mastercard)	26.6
35 Northern Bank (Visa/Mastercard)	26.8
36 Co-operative Classic (Visa)	26.8
37 Standard Chartered (Visa)	29.8

Source: Moneyfacts (*Independent on Sunday*, 12 September 1993).

in order, with the bank with the lowest interest rate at the top and the bank with the highest rate at the bottom. This makes the extraction of relevant information easier.

The next example is slightly more complex. It is taken from a piece of educational research carried out on the West Indian island of St. Eustace. Here we are just presenting a table, and we will analyse the data more thoroughly in Chapter 12.

Each script was given an impression mark ranging from 1 (low) to 5 (high). Table 4.3 shows the frequencies of scripts awarded each impression mark. The entries in the rows and the columns are numbers. The first column tells you what marks were achieved. The second column tells you the number of scripts that achieved each mark and the third column the percentage of scripts that achieved each mark.

Table 4.3 Frequency of impression marks in schools in St. Eustace (1 = low, 5 = high)

Impression mark	Frequency	Percentage
1	39	13
2	75	25
3	108	36
4	48	16
5	30	10

Graphs

A graph is a way of showing relationships between data. They can often be drawn straight from a table of data. For example, we might have figures giving the prices of second-hand cars. Table 4.4 shows the relationship between the price of Amalgamated Motors Turkeys and their age.

Table 4.4 Price of second-hand Turkeys by year

	Year of manufacture									
	1984	1985	1986	1987	1988	1989	1990	1991	1992	1993
Current retail price (£)	900	1100	1200	1300	1700	2200	3000	4000	5500	8000

This can be drawn as a graph with two variables, one representing year of manufacture and the other price. Once the graph is drawn, it is easy to see that there is a relationship between the age of the car and its current price.

By plotting a graph it is possible to visualize this relationship. The two variables, date and price, can be plotted along the vertical and horizontal axes of the graph; it is usual to put time along the horizontal axis. It is also possible to construct a multiple graph where, for example, you can compare the relationship between age and price of several makes of car. The graph is shown in Fig. 4.1.

Similar figures for Siesta cars are given in Table 4.5. If you plot these figures on the same graph as the Turkeys, you will be able to compare the depreciation of the two cars.

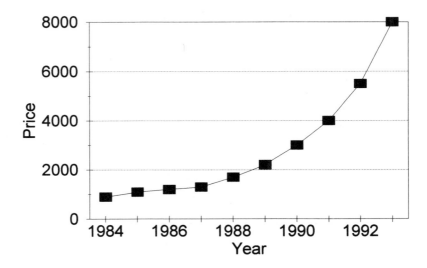

Figure 4.1   Price of Turkeys

Table 4.5   Price of second-hand Siestas by year

	Year of manufacture									
	1984	*1985*	*1986*	*1987*	*1988*	*1989*	*1990*	*1991*	*1992*	*1993*
Current retail price (£)	1600	2000	2400	2900	3400	3900	4500	5100	6200	7500

STATISTICAL DIAGRAMS

Statistical diagrams are used to give a visual representation of data. Data are often easier to understand if they are presented in pictorial form. Statistical diagrams can do this. Suppose we have sorted our data into groups. We can illustrate the numbers in each group in different ways.

Bar charts

In a bar chart, the number in each group is represented by the length of its bar. This sort of diagram often appears in newspapers to illustrate economic figures. In the example in Fig. 4.2, the corn harvest for a European country in the nineteenth century is illustrated for the years 1820–28.

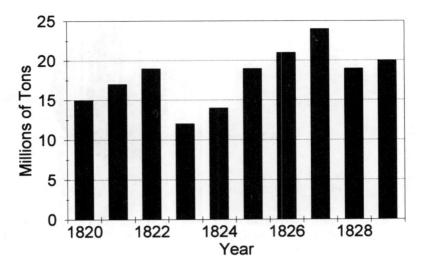

Figure 4.2 Corn harvest

Pie charts

Another commonly used sort of diagram is the pie chart, in which the number in each group is represented by the angle in its slice of pie (for which the technical term is *sector*). This sort of diagram is very good at giving relative sizes. They are a very useful way of comparing relative proportions, for example, of expenditure on different items. Table 4.6 shows the expenditure of a local authority, as divided into groups such as education, housing, roads, etc.

Table 4.6 Local authority expenditure, 1993

Service	£ (m)
Education	150
Housing	80
Roads	40
Leisure	20
Total	290

The total expenditure was £290 million. The expenditure on roads was £40 million, which represents $\frac{40}{290} = \frac{4}{29}$ of the whole. So the angle in the roads sector should be $\frac{4}{29} \times 360 = 49.7°$. The angles for the other sectors are found

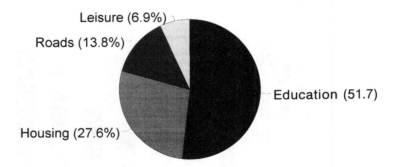

Figure 4.3 Expenditure for 1993

similarly. The pie chart is shown in Fig. 4.3. This sort of diagram is especially good for comparing groups. But it gives the relative sizes of the groups. We cannot find the *actual* sizes without more information.

Suppose the figures for the borough for the following year are as given in Table 4.7. Notice that all the sums have increased by 50%. But the *relative* sums have remained constant, so the pie chart for this year will be the same as for the previous year (Fig. 4.4).

Table 4.7 Local authority expenditure, 1994

Service	£ (m)
Education	225
Housing	120
Roads	60
Leisure	30
Total	435

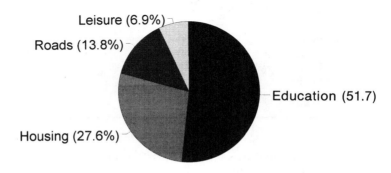

Figure 4.4 Expenditure for 1994

In order to compare absolute expenditure between the two years, a bar chart would be more useful. Figure 4.5 is a bar chart showing this information.

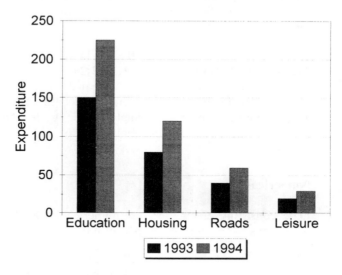

Figure 4.5 Expenditure for 1993 and 1994

DIFFERENT KINDS OF DATA

There are several different types of data. Information could consist of names, numbers, dates, and so on. Dates are classified by the mathematical operations (if any) that can be performed on them.

Nominal

Nominal data have no mathematical content at all. So there are no mathematical operations to be performed. Examples of nominal scales include the following:

Sex	male–female
Names	Jones–Davies–Rees–Williams–Hopkins
Colour of eyes	blue–brown–grey–green
Ethnicity	European–Afro-Caribbean–Asian–Chinese

Ordinal

Ordinal data show properties arranged according to *rank*. The ordering is itself a mathematical arrangement. Examples of ordinal scales include the following:

Exam grades	A B C D E
Degree classifications	1st 2:1 2:2 3rd Pass
School classes	Year 1 Year 2 Year 3 Year 4 Year 5
Orders of preference	1st 2nd 3rd 4th 5th
Questionnaire opinion	Strongly agree Agree No opinion Disagree Strongly disagree

Numerical

Data consisting of numbers are numerical data. We can apply numerical operations to the data. Examples of numerical scales include the following.

> Intelligence quotient
> Reading age
> Temperature scale
> Weight
> Height
> Age
> Income

We need to emphasize the difference between ordinal and numerical data. Numerical data are ordinal as well, as a set of numbers can be arranged in increasing or decreasing order. But the reverse is not true – ordinal data are not necessarily numerical. The exam grades are placed in order, but they are not numbers and arithmetic cannot be performed on them. Even if the grades were given as numbers, it would not really make sense to add the first and the third grades together.

Exercises   Classify the following data as nominal, ordinal or numerical:

(a) Manchester   Liverpool   Leeds   London
(b) Wind strength from 1 (low) to 10 (very high)
(c) Life-expectancy
(d) Unemployment figures
(e) Years before the birth of Christ
(f) Family relationships: father   mother   brother   sister   cousin   uncle
                           aunt   niece   nephew

MEASURES OF CENTRAL TENDENCY

Suppose our statistical data consist of numbers. An *average* is a single number which somehow gives an idea of where the central point of all the other numbers are. This is sometimes poshly called a *measure of central tendency*.

The *mean* is what people normally understand by the word average. To find the mean of 10 numbers, add them up and divide by 10.

Example   The eight children who took a test obtained the following marks:

15   14   18   63   20   19   15   20

The sum of all these numbers is 184. So the mean is 184 ÷ 8 = 23.

The *median* is an average that refers to the order of the data. Suppose the data are written in increasing order. The median will be the middle item – half the numbers are greater than it and half smaller.

Look at the numbers above, for which we found a mean of 23. Notice that seven out of the eight children got less than this score – the mean was distorted by one very able (or very dishonest) pupil. The mean does not give much indication of the performance of the class as a whole.

In these circumstances, the median is a much better average from which to evaluate the class. List the marks in increasing order:

14   15   15   18   19   20   20   63

The two middle numbers are 18 and 19. Take halfway between them, to obtain a median of 18.5. We can see that four children did better than this score and four worse.

If scores are repeated, we can still find the median. Let us say the scores are:

5 7 3 5 8 2 7 4 6 2 5 4 3 6 3 5 6 3 6 4 5

Arranging these in increasing order:

2 2 3 3 3 3 4 4 4 5 5 5 5 5 6 6 6 6 7 7 8

Here we have 21 numbers. The eleventh is a 5. We say that the median is 5, even though it is not strictly true to say that half the numbers are less than 5 and half greater.

The median can be applied to ordinal as well as numerical data. Suppose that the scores were given as grades, instead of numbers. Say they were:

A B A C D B C E D C B E A B C D E A C C B

Arranging in decreasing alphabetic order:

E   E   E   D   D   D   C   C   C   C   C   B   B   B   B   B   A   A   A   A

Here we have 21 grades, of which the eleventh is a C. So we can say, as above, that the median grade is C.

Notice that we could not find the mean grade. It makes no sense to add letters and divide by 21.

There is a third sort of average. The *mode* is the most commonly occurring item. In the examples above, the mode score was 5, and the mode grade was C. The mode is useful for showing when there is a peak in the data, e.g. at what age unemployment is at a maximum or what is the most common type of accommodation lived in by students.

Data do not have to be nominal or even ordinal for us to find their mode. If we have a collection of Christian names, we can find the most common one, which will be the modal name. It would make no sense to find the mean or median name.

Exercises   The following are the numbers of people in different social class groups in a small European country:

Upper class	1 million
Upper middle class	2 million
Middle class 1	4 million
Middle class 2	5 million
Skilled working class	6 million
Semi-skilled working class	7 million
Unskilled working class	3 million
Unemployed	1 million

(a) What type of data are these?
(b) What is the modal class?
(c) Can you find the median class?
(d) Can you find the mean class?

Frequency tables

Suppose the data are presented in the form of a frequency table. Then we can still find the three averages. Suppose the table is of numbers of children per family, as in Table 4.8.

Adding up the frequencies, there are 140 families here. The total number of children is found by multiplying each number by its frequency and then adding, as in:

Table 4.8 Numbers of children per family

	No. of children								
	0	*1*	*2*	*3*	*4*	*5*	*6*	*7*	*8+*
Frequency	23	25	42	23	16	8	2	1	0

$$0 \times 23 + 1 \times 25 + 2 \times 42 + 3 \times 23 + 4 \times 16 + 5 \times 8 + 6 \times 2 + 7 \times 1$$
$$+ 8 \times 0 = 301$$

So the mean number of children is $301 \div 140 = 2.15$ children per family.

For the median, we imagine that all the numbers were laid out in a row. There would be 23 0's, followed by 25 1's, 42 2's, and so on. The middle two numbers would be the 70th and the 71st. Both of these numbers would be 2's. So the median family size is 2.

The mode requires no calculation. Looking at Table 4.8, the largest frequency is 42. Hence the mode family size is 2.

Exercises   Table 4.9 lists the numbers of adolescent children in the population of a country.

Table 4.9 Number of children per age per 10,000 of the population

	Age to nearest year						
	10	*11*	*12*	*13*	*14*	*15*	*16*
No. of children	200	300	100	100	400	500	600

(a) What is the mode age?
(b) What is the mean age of the children?

Dispersion

The averages of the previous section tell us where the central point of the data is. This may not be the only thing we need to know about the data. For example, we might have two countries with the same average income. But the countries might differ greatly in the degree of equality of income – one with a large difference between the incomes of rich and poor, and the other with most people receiving roughly the same amount of money. So we often want to know how closely the data are clustered around the central point. A measure of the closeness is called a *measure of dispersion*.

Suppose we have already found the mean *m*. Then one way of measuring the dispersion is to find the average difference from the mean. The measure is called the *mean deviation*. On page 57 we gave 8 marks achieved in a test. To find the mean deviation of the 8 marks above, note that we have already found the mean to be 23. The differences from 23 are:

$$8 \quad 9 \quad 5 \quad 40 \quad 3 \quad 4 \quad 8 \quad 3$$

The average of these numbers is 10. So the mean deviation is 10.

This is a very sensible and natural way to measure dispersion. Unfortunately, it is very difficult to handle mathematically. The trouble is that some of the numbers are greater than the mean and some less, and the averaging process has to take account of this. The most commonly used measure of dispersion is as follows.

Having found the mean, find the difference of each number from the mean and *square* it. Then the result will be positive, regardless of whether the number was less than the mean or greater. Average these squared differences, and the result will be the *variance*.

So suppose we have 4 items of data, *a*, *b*, *c* and *d*, and that their mean is *m*. The variance will be:

$$\frac{(a - m)^2 + (b - m)^2 + (c - m)^2 + (d - m)^2}{4}$$

The variance measures the dispersion of the data. Sometimes we give the variance directly, sometimes we take its square root, called the *standard deviation*. For the marks above, we have already found their differences from the mean. The squared differences are:

$$8^2 = 64 \quad 9^2 = 81 \quad 5^2 = 25 \quad 40^2 = 1600 \quad 3^2 = 9 \quad 4^2 = 16 \quad 8^2 = 64 \quad 32^2 = 9$$

Average these eight squared differences, and we obtain 233.5. The square root of this is 15.3. So the variance is 233.5, and the standard deviation 15.3.

Exercise   Machine tools gradually improved in accuracy during the course of the nineteenth century. A certain sort of lathe was used to make flywheels for factory machinery. Table 4.10 below gives the diameters in feet of eight flywheels produced at different stages in the century.

Table 4.10   Diameters of flywheels in the nineteenth century

Year	Diameter (ft)							
1835	3.01	3.02	2.99	2.99	3.01	3.02	2.98	2.98
1865	3.005	2.997	2.996	3.002	3.004	2.999	2.998	2.999

(a) Find the mean diameter for both years.
(b) Find the mean deviation for both years.
(c) Find the variance for both years.
(d) What conclusions can you draw?

CORRELATION

In many situations, we want to know whether two things are connected. A measure for the degree of connection is called a *measure of correlation*. As with dispersion, there are many ways we could define correlation. The one most often used is the *product–moment correlation coefficient*, or just correlation coefficient for short.

The correlation coefficient and similar measures are widely used in the social sciences. Very often sociologists, psychologists and others are concerned to see whether or not there is a relationship between two variables, such as crime and poverty, personality type and job satisfaction, stress levels and incidence of disease. The correlation coefficient is a handy way of indicating whether or not such a relationship exists.

Suppose we have n pairs of values (x_1, y_1), (x_2, y_2), and so on up to (x_n, y_n). Let us suppose that the mean of the x-values is $\bar{x}$ and of the y-values $\bar{y}$, and that the standard deviations are σ_x and σ_y, respectively. The formula for the correlation coefficient is:

$$\rho = \frac{\Sigma x_i y_i - n\bar{x}\bar{y}}{n\sigma_x \sigma_y}$$

x-values	1	2	3	4	5	6	7	8
y-values	32	41	42	52	50	61	69	92

By work in the previous sections, we find that $\bar{x} = 4.5$ and $\bar{y} = 54.875$. The standard deviations are $\sigma_x = 2.29$ and $\sigma_y = 17.8$. The $\Sigma x_i y_i$ is found by multiplying each pair of terms and adding, to obtain:

$$1 \times 32 + 2 \times 41 + 3 \times 42 + 4 \times 52 + 5 \times 50 + 6 \times 61 + 7 \times 69 + 8 \times 92$$
$$= 2283$$

Now put all the values into the formula.

$$\rho = \frac{2283 - 8 \times 4.5 \times 54.875}{8 \times 2.29 \times 17.8} = 0.944$$

This is just a number. What does it mean? It can be shown that the correlation coefficient lies between -1 and 1. A value of 1 implies that the variables x and y are perfectly correlated, so that if we plotted them on a graph they would lie on a straight line as shown in Fig. 4.6. A value of -1

implies they are perfectly negatively correlated, so that the plotted points lie on a line sloping downhill as shown in Fig. 4.7.

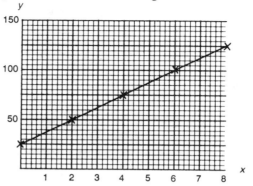

Figure 4.6

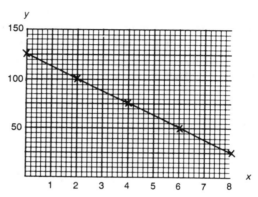

Figure 4.7

A graph of our eight points is shown in Fig. 4.8. Notice that they do lie roughly on a straight line, but not perfectly so. Hence the correlation coefficient is a little bit less than 1.

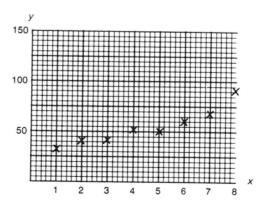

Figure 4.8

If two variables are not connected in any way, then the correlation coefficient between them is 0. The diagram showing uncorrelated variables could be like that shown in Fig. 4.9.

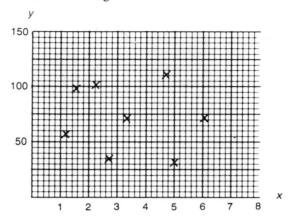

Figure 4.9

Exercises   (a) One of the reasons that is often given for giving large pay rises to directors, is that good past performance will be rewarded and the directors will thus be motivated to perform well in future in order that they will continue to be rewarded in this way. It should be possible to see whether or not there is a positive correlation of directors' pay increases with company profitability. Table 4.11 allows for an inspection to be made. It shows the rise or fall in profits of 6 companies and the salary increase of their directors. Find the correlation coefficient between the salary increase and profit increase.

Table 4.11   Average salary increases for the directors of certain companies together with the percentage rise or fall in profits over the previous year (1992–93)

Company	Salary increase (%)	Year's profit rise/fall (%)
1. Carlton Communications	42.5	15.2
2. North West Water	35.4	7.0
3. Kingfisher	33.3	−16.5
4. Anglian Water	29.9	12.3
5. Lasmo	28.5	−85.77
6. Guinness	24.3	−11.7

Source: The Independent, 9 September 1993.

(b) Educationists would be interested in whether or not there was a relationship between IQ and success in examinations. Table 4.12 gives the results for 10 children. Find the correlation coefficient for this table.

Table 4.12 Pupils' IQ and examination scores ($n = 10$)

IQ	Examination score
130	80
128	72
122	62
118	60
116	52
114	60
110	56
106	50
104	52
100	48

LINEAR REGRESSION

In the section on correlation, we considered cases when two measurements were applied to our subjects, and we found a correlation coefficient to measure how closely these measurements were connected. With a high (close to 1) correlation coefficient, the points corresponding to the information lie roughly on a straight line with positive slope. Suppose we draw this straight line. Then we can use it to predict other values. This procedure is known as *linear regression*.

Let us suppose that we have plotted out pairs of values (x_1, y_1), (x_2, y_2), and so on up to (x_n, y_n). We could try fitting the straight line by hand, but this would be very unreliable. We need a mathematical way of calculating the line which best fits the points. This line would minimize in some way the differences between the y-values on the line and the y-values of the points. The method favoured by statisticians is called the *method of least squares*, and it minimizes the sum of the squares of these differences.

The method leads to the following formula for the line of best fit:

$$y = ax + b, \quad \text{where } a = \frac{\Sigma x_i y_i - n\bar{x}\bar{y}}{\Sigma x_i^2 - n\bar{x}^2} \quad \text{and } b = \bar{y} - a\bar{x}$$

You do not have to know how this formula is obtained. Notice though that the formula giving b ensures that the line goes through the point $(\bar{x}, \bar{y})$ of the mean values of both x and y.

Let us find the line of regression for the x- and y-values given on page 61. Virtually all of the calculation has been done already, in working out the correlation coefficent of the variables. We know that:

$$\bar{x} = 4.5 \quad \bar{y} = 54.875 \quad \Sigma x^2 = 204 \quad \Sigma xy = 2283$$

Put these into the formula:

$$a = \frac{2283 - 8 \times 4.5 \times 54.875}{204 - 8 \times 4.5^2} = 7.32 \quad b = 54.875 - 7.32 \times 4.5 = 21.9$$

So our line is $y = 7.32x + 21.9$ (Fig. 4.10). Once we have this formula, we can use it to predict other values. We could predict that for $x = 9$, the value of y is:

$$7.32 \times 9 + 21.9 = 87.78$$

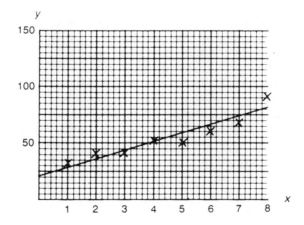

Figure 4.10

Exercises Table 4.13 gives the proportion of owner-occupiers in 10 constituencies, along with the proportion of support for the Conservative Party.

(a) Find the line of regression giving C (Conservative support) in terms of P (Proportion of owner-occupiers).

Table 4.13   Owner-occupiers and support for the Conservative Party in 10 constituencies

	Constituencies									
	1	*2*	*3*	*4*	*5*	*6*	*7*	*8*	*9*	*10*
Owner-occupiers (%)	40	53	62	68	36	44	59	66	50	72
Conservative support (%)	18	39	59	66	28	48	50	30	46	70

(b) Another constituency has a proportion of owner-occupiers of 45%. What do you predict will be its level of Conservative support?

Multiple regression

The real value of regression in social science research lies in its ability to plot the influence of one factor on another. For example, suppose we examine the link between smoking and lung cancer. We would have two variables, the *number of cigarettes smoked* and the *incidence of lung cancer*. We are investigating whether or not smoking causes lung cancer. Nobody would seriously suggest that it is the other way round, that lung cancer causes smoking. So the incidence of cancer is dependent on the number of cigarettes smoked. We say that the number of cigarettes is the *independent* variable, and that the incidence of cancer is the *dependent* variable.

It is not often that there is one single cause of a phenomenon. Often there will be many independent variables which might affect the dependent variable. Regression with more than one variable allows the effects of more than one factor to be assessed. The technique is known as *multiple regression* and is frequently used in social science research. The process is usually carried out by computer, since the calculation of multiple regression equations is very complex and time-consuming if done by hand.

To give an example of how it is used, consider the relationship between lung cancer and smoking. A serious medical researcher would want to know far more about possible causes of lung cancer, other than smoking, and would like to know how they relate to each other. She may well wish to examine the joint effects of smoking, the presence of the radioactive gas, radon, in homes, atmospheric pollution, to name a few of the possibilities. In order to examine all these possibilities together, she would need to construct an equation with five independent variables like this:

$$I = aC + bR + cP + d$$

Here I is the incidence, C is the number of cigarettes smoked, R the level of radon, P the pollution level. The numbers a, b, c and d are constants which are to be found.

There are different ways of carrying out a multiple regression, but the point for you to realize at this stage is that it is an important analytical tool that allows social scientists and historians to examine various possible causal factors.

Exercise   Multiple regression might be used to predict the level of support for a particular political party. Make a list of five independent variables which would affect the proportion of people who vote Conservative in a given constituency.

CASE STUDY: ELECTIONS

Political elections provide a rich souce of material for statistical description and analysis. Table 4.14 gives the general election results for the main political parties in Great Britain as a whole, between 1950 and 1974. The statistical operations that you will be asked to perform will have a definite political moral.

Table 4.14   General election results in Great Britain 1950–74

Year	Party	No. of votes	No. of seats
1950	Conservative	12,502,567	298
	Liberal	2,621,548	9
	Labour	13,266,592	315
1951	Conservative	13,717,538	321
	Liberal	730,556	6
	Labour	13,948,605	295
1955	Conservative	13,286,569	344
	Liberal	722,405	6
	Labour	12,404,970	277
1959	Conservative	13,749,830	365
	Liberal	1,638,571	6
	Labour	12,215,538	258
1964	Conservative	12,001,396	304
	Liberal	3,092,878	9
	Labour	12,205,814	317
1966	Conservative	11,418,433	253
	Liberal	2,327,533	12
	Labour	13,064,951	363
1970	Conservative	13,145,123	330
	Liberal	2,117,035	6
	Labour	12,179,341	287
1974 (Feb.)	Conservative	11,868,906	297
	Liberal	6,603,470	14
	Labour	11,639,243	301

(a) Draw graphs showing support for the three parties over these years.
(b) Draw bar charts showing support for the three parties in 1974.
(c) Draw two pie charts, one showing the votes for the parties in 1974, the other showing the seats gained in that year. What can you conclude?
(d) For each party, find the mean number of votes.
(e) For the Labour Party, find the correlation coefficient between the votes and the number of seats won.
(f) Find the linear regression equation giving the number of Labour votes in terms of the year. From your equation, predict the Labour vote in 1987. (In fact it was 10,029,807.)

5   Statistical inference

The science of statistics – like some branches of alternative medicine – has always had a rather murky reputation. People sometimes greet its results with scepticism, saying 'Oh, you can prove anything by statistics' or the like.

The fault lies not in the subject itself, but in those who interpret it. It is easy to exploit the widely held prejudice that a fact expressed in hard numbers must be true, by presenting a statistical result as if it embodied an absolute truth. There is an excellent book on this, *How to Lie with Statistics* (Darrell Huff, Penguin, 1991), which shows how simple it is to present numerical data in such a way that it is misleading or downright false.

This chapter is about statistical proof. The word 'proof' is used in different ways by different people. It might be well to distinguish between these.

A A mathematician proves a theorem.
B A chemist proves that a substance is composed out of certain elements.
C A statistician proves that there is a connection between diet and a certain disease.

A A mathematical proof consists of logical reasoning. It does not involve any physical experiment. If the logical steps are correct (which requires checking by other mathematicians) then there is no doubt about the truth of the theorem. Pythagoras' Theorem, for example, has been proved absolutely, and no sensible person is able to deny its truth.
B A chemical proof does involve experiment, for example to find the concentration of nitrogen in the air. But provided the experiment has been correctly carried out (and duplicated by other chemists), there is no doubt about the conclusion. No sensible person will be able to deny its truth.
C A statistical proof also involves experiment. But there is a radical difference in what the statistician is trying to prove. The mathematician proves that the theorem is always true. The chemist proves that every pure sample of air is made up of a certain proportion of nitrogen. But the statistician is not claiming that every person who eats certain foods will contract the disease. There will always be exceptions – some people who eat the food will avoid the disease, and some people who do not

eat the food will contract the disease. All that the statistician claims is that there is a connection between diet and disease – that if you eat the food, then you are more likely to get the disease.

So however many people the statistician tests, the result will never be proved absolutely. It will always be possible for a sensible person (perhaps the manufacturer of the food under suspicion) to deny that there is a connection.

So any statement of the form 'Statistics have proved that ...', must be treated with caution. Statistics can never prove anything absolutely. The strongest conclusion that can be reached by statistics is that something is very likely, never that it is certain. And this assumes, of course, that the facts on which the statistical conclusion is based are themselves true.

BIAS AND STATISTICAL ERROR

Suppose we collect a great mass of data and calculate the mean, median, standard deviation, and so on, by the methods of the previous chapter. What conclusions can be reached from the data, and how sure can we be that they are correct? There are two reasons why we should be wary of jumping hastily to conclusions derived from data.

1. *Bias*: We must be sure that the data collected represent fairly the thing that we are trying to measure. If they don't, then the data and the conclusions will be *biased*, unless we take steps to compensate for this.
2. *Statistical error*: However much data we collect, we can never be absolutely sure that they represent the whole situation accurately, unless they contain all the information available. There is always the possibility that, just by chance, the figures we have collected are exceptional in some way. This is *statistical error*.

Some examples might be helpful.

An opinion poll before an election aims to predict the outcome of the election by asking a sample of people what their voting intentions are. The opinion poll could be biased for the following reasons:

1. It was conducted in one part of the country only, or from one age group only, or in any situation where supporters of one party were likely to be unfairly represented. There is a famous example of this in the USA, in which the outcome of the 1936 Roosevelt–Landon Presidential election was predicted on the basis of a poll conducted by telephone. Of course, at that time, only the richer section of society could afford telephones. The poll did not take account of this, and gave a completely inaccurate prediction of who would win the election.
2. The person who did the polling influenced people to answer in one way rather than another. After all, a lot of people do not make their minds

up before election day, and may respond to a pollster in the way in which they think the pollster wants to hear. If the pollster is dressed in a smart business suit, then the people questioned may be influenced to respond more favourably towards the business-oriented party.

3. The opinion poll questions themselves may influence people to respond one way rather than another. A polling question of the form 'Do you think more money should be spent on hospitals, or would you vote for the Reactionary Party?', will elicit a biased response.

Even if great care has been taken to ensure that the opinion poll is as unbiased as is possible, its results are never 100% reliable. Suppose the poll reports 55% support for Party A and 45% for Party B. If only 20 people were questioned, then the information is almost useless. No reliable conclusions can be reached about the voting intentions of the electorate as a whole from the fact that of 20 people questioned, 11 said they would vote for Party A. We cannot conclude that Party A will win the next election.

The same principle applies even when the sample is larger. Even if an opinion poll of 1000 people registers 55% support for Party A, it is always possible that the sample contained, just by chance, an abnormally high proportion of Party A supporters. We cannot conclude for certain that Party A is supported by a majority of the electorate, merely that it is very likely that this is the case. Any random sample is liable to this statistical error.

Another important type of bias may arise when the sample is self-selecting. A case might be where a woman's magazine invites its readers to write in and say whether or not they are satisfied with their relationships. It is possible that those who are dissatisfied with their relationships will be more likely to write than those who are not.

Self-selected samples have played an important role in social research and the consequences have been far-reaching. Only now are we beginning to see the degree of bias that such methods can produce. In the 1940s, Kinsey and Martin conducted a survey of the sexual behaviour of Americans. The data were obtained from people who had volunteered to be interviewed. One of their best known findings, which has been accepted as accurate by most non-experts for years, is that one in twenty of the male population is homosexual. There have been more recent reports on sexual behaviour in the USA and comparable European countries. Sociologists are now more rigorous about how they obtain their data, and the new surveys did not rely on self-selection of interviewees. The new studies agree on a figure of about one in a hundred is homosexual rather than one in twenty.

Examples   Here are five examples which will continue throughout the chapter. In each case, think about how the statistical information could be biased, or subject to statistical error.

A   Heated driving seats have been introduced into Amalgamated Motors' range of Siesta cars as an optional extra. A motoring organization is concerned about the safety aspect of these accessories. The organization conducts a survey to find the accident rate of 1000 motorists who have these seats in their cars. This is then compared with the national accident rate for these cars.

B   A school wants to encourage its pupils to work hard. One teacher is delegated to collect data on 20 pupils. The teacher finds the correlation coefficient between the number of hours of study and the mark in the end-of-year exam.

C   A new medicine for ME is developed. The pharmaceutical firm test it on two groups of 50 sufferers each. The first group is given the real drug, the other group receives a placebo, which has no active ingredient. None of the patients know whether they are receiving the real medicine or the placebo. All the patients are asked whether they feel any better, and the proportions of the two groups who answer positively are compared.

D   A sociologist claims that tastes in music are connected with disposable income. Thirty people are ranked in order by income. Each person is then asked whether he or she is a fan of the country singer Waylon Anguish.

E   There is continual debate about methods of teaching reading. Data are collected on 200 pupils, and a table is drawn up to see the effect of the teaching method on whether the pupils were classified as good readers by the age of eight.

These five examples will be fully analysed in the next chapter.

POPULATIONS AND SAMPLES

In this section, we will look at an important distinction for work in statistics. A *population* is the collection of the things that the scientist or the statistician wishes to study. It is the collection which he is interested in, even though he will not be able to examine every individual. A *sample*, on the other hand, is a selection from the population which is small enough to be studied. To be useful, the sample has got to represent the population accurately in the properties which are of interest to the investigator.

One of the main – although by no means the only – reasons why inference using probability statements is so widely used in the social sciences is that it is practically impossible to look at and measure every individual in a population. It is not usually possible, for example, to ask everyone in the country how they intend to vote in the next general election or what brand of washing powder they prefer. The government does periodically collect a certain amount of data on everyone by means of a series of questionnaires and interviews known as a *census*. The census is so expensive to conduct, however, that only a government would have the resources to do it, and even then the amount and kind of information gathered is of a limited nature.

It is much more common for research organizations to collect data from a small proportion of a population and then to *infer* conclusions about the population.

Random and stratified samples

The sample has got to represent accurately on a small scale the characteristics of the population in which the researcher is interested. One way of selecting a fair sample is by picking representatives at random. This is a *random* sample. A random sample for an opinion poll could be found by programming a computer to go through the electoral register and to pick each name with probability 1 in 30,000. If there are 30 million registered voters, then this will result in a randomly selected sample of 1000 voters.

Another way of selecting the sample is by splitting up the population into groups and selecting people at random within those groups. This is a *stratified* sample. A stratified sample for an opinion poll might divide the population by sex, region and class. The samplers would then ensure that the sample contained a representative number of, for example, upper-class women from Scotland.

DRAWING CONCLUSIONS

We might want a definite answer (subject of course to statistical error) to a definite question. In the example of the opinion poll above, the question would be: 'Which party is supported by the majority of the electorate?' Putting it another way: 'Is Party A supported by more than 50% of the electorate?'

It is never enough to argue that: 'More than 50% of the sample supported Party A, therefore more than 50% of the electorate supports Party A'. The analysis of the result must take account of how large the sample was.

We hope to be able to draw a conclusion, subject as always to a probability reservation. There are many cases like this in statistics, and there is a special vocabulary to deal with them.

In the physical sciences, we can often draw a conclusion without any reservations. After conducting a chemical experiment, we can conclude that: 'This substance contains carbon', not 'with probability 0.95 this chemical contains carbon'. But in the social or medical sciences this is not always so clear. Suppose our claim is that eating red peppers leads to throat cancer. There are people who eat red peppers who don't get cancers, and there are people with cancers who have never eaten red peppers, but the claim is that:

'On the whole, those who eat red peppers are more likely to contract cancer'. It is necessary to state unambiguously what we are trying to prove or disprove.

So a social or medical scientist puts forward a theory. It might be that Party A is supported by a majority of the electorate, or that eating red peppers leads to throat cancer, or the like. Data are then collected, and the theory is tested by the data. There is now an important distinction to be made, about two sorts of hypotheses:

H_0 The null hypothesis is that there is no conclusion to be reached in the matter under consideration. It is that neither party has a lead in the election, or that eating red peppers has no effect whatsoever on one's chances of contracting cancer. Notice that the null hypothesis is precise: it is that Party A's support is exactly 50%, or that a red-pepper-eater has exactly the same probability of contracting cancer as a non-red-pepper-eater. Because the null hypothesis is precise, statistical calculations can be based upon it.

H_1 The alternative hypothesis, or research hypothesis, is the theory that the scientist is trying to establish. It is the theory that Party A is ahead in the election race, or that red peppers lead to cancer. It is usually imprecise – we are not guessing the amount by which Party A is ahead, or the exact extent of the danger of eating red peppers.

An analogy with a court of law may be helpful here. When a defendant is brought before a court of law, the theory of the prosecution is that she is guilty of the offence. This is the alternative hypothesis. The defence's hypothesis, that she is not guilty, is the null hypothesis. In English law, a defendant is innocent until proved guilty. It is up to the prosecution to prove that the accused did commit the crime, it is not up to the defence to prove that she didn't. In other words, the prosecution needs to prove the alternative hypothesis, thus disproving the null hypothesis. If the prosecution fails to prove its case, then the defence wins and the defendant is pronounced not guilty. This means that the null hypothesis is retained; it does not necessarily mean that the null hypothesis is proved.

When doing a statistical test, it is up to the tester to prove that the alternative hypothesis is true – that Party A is ahead in the election race, that peppers do lead to cancer. No-one is required to prove the null hypothesis – indeed, it would be impossible to prove that two parties have *exactly* the same level of support, or that people with different diets have *exactly* the same risk of contracting a particular disease. So the burden of proof rests on the proponents of the alternative hypothesis, and unless this is proved the null hypothesis is retained.

Examples   Here we continue the examples which were introduced earlier. Look back at page 72, and for each of the five cases **A**–**E** write down the null and alternative hypotheses. We will illustrate this by going through the first example.

Suppose that the average accident rate for the Siesta is 0.2 per annum. This means that 20 out of 100 Siestas have an accident in any one year. The null hypothesis is that Siestas fitted with heated driving seats also have an accident rate of 0.2. The alternative hypothesis is that the accident rate for these Siestas is different from 0.2.

The mathematical symbolization for this is as follows. The accident rate for all Siestas is 0.2. We often call this μ_0. The accident rate for the cars fitted with heated seats is μ, and it is this that we wish to investigate. The null hypothesis can be written as:

$$H_0 : \mu = \mu_0$$

The alternative hypothesis can be written as:

$$H_1 : \mu \neq \mu_0$$

If the null hypothesis is false, then the alternative hypothesis must be true.

ERRORS

It must always be held in mind that statistical conclusions are subject to a probabilistic reservation. The conclusions may be wrong. In the case of a test, there are two ways in which the conclusion can be wrong.

1. *Type I error*: Wrongly accepting the alternative hypothesis. For the examples above, this would be concluding that Party A was ahead in electoral support when it wasn't, or in concluding that eating red peppers leads to cancer when it doesn't.
2. *Type II error*: Wrongly rejecting the alternative hypothesis. For the examples above, this would be failing to conclude that Party A is ahead when it is, or of failing to establish a link between red peppers and cancer.

To continue the analogy with a court of law, recall that the alternative hypothesis is that the defendant is guilty of the crime she is accused of. At the end of the trial, the verdict is given: if it is 'guilty' the prosecution will have proved the alternative hypothesis, and if it is 'not guilty' they will have failed to prove it. Note that the defence have not proved the null hypothesis of innocence – under English law that is not required of the defence. In law as in statistics, it is hardly ever possible to prove things with absolute certainty. We can never be absolutely certain that the verdict of the jury is the correct one. The prosecution has got to satisfy the jury that the accused is guilty beyond reasonable doubt. Even in a well-conducted trial, it is always possible that a horrible miscarriage of justice has occurred. What the law does require is that a rational person would have sufficent reason to believe that the accused is guilty.

If a Type I error has been made, then the alternative hypothesis has been wrongly accepted. If a Type II error has been made, then the null hypothesis has been wrongly retained. In terms of law:

Type I error: convicting an innocent woman.
Type II error: acquitting a guilty woman.

Both these errors have bad consequences. If a Type I error is made in a trial, then an innocent woman may have her life ruined for a crime committed by someone else. If a Type II error is made, then a criminal is freed, perhaps to repeat the same crime.

In English law, the first error is thought by far the worst, so it is said that we would release 100 criminals rather than convict one innocent person. In statistical jargon, the probability of a Type II error should be 100 times the probability of a Type I error.

Examples   Look at the five examples above. In each case write down what would be a Type I error and a Type II error.

To continue with our case of the cars with heated driving seats.

● *Type I Error*: To say that the cars with the heated driving seats are more dangerous than the average when they are not.
● *Type II Error*: To say that cars with heated driving seats are as safe as the average when in fact they are either safer or more dangerous than the average.

COST OF ERRORS

In the law analogy, we pointed out that there is always a possibility of making an error, and that the Type II error was less bad than the Type I error. When doing a statistical test there are costs, financial or otherwise, to both of the errors, and the test is arranged to take account of these costs.

A factory will regularly test samples of its products. It may not be able to test them all, either for reasons of cost or because the testing procedure may destroy the product. If a sample fails the test, then the whole of the batch from which it came may be abandoned. Let us consider two examples:

1 Testing climbing ropes, whose breaking strength should be 200 kg.
2 Testing violin strings, whose breaking strength should be 20 kg.

In both cases, the null hypothesis is that the batch is good, i.e. that the breaking strength is what it is claimed to be. The alternative hypothesis is that the breaking strength is less than the claimed amount. (We need not worry if the strength is *greater* than claimed.)

If a Type I error is made in either case, then we will wrongly accept the alternative hypothesis, i.e. we will assume that the batch is substandard when in fact it is perfectly good. This might mean that the whole day's production would be lost, which would cost the firm a lot of money.

If a Type II error is made, then we will wrongly retain the null hypothesis, i.e. we will assume that the batch is adequate, when in fact it is substandard. What will the result be? The consequences for example **1** could be disastrous – the factory will release onto the market rope which may not be capable of supporting the weight of the climber. The results could be fatal. For example **2**, though, a Type II error is not so serious. If a violin string snaps in the middle of a concert it will distract the audience, but no greater injury will ensue than a nasty sting on the violinist's cheek.

So for example **1**, the factory will make the probability of a Type II error very low indeed, by testing a large number of ropes and having stringent conditions for acceptance of the batch. For example **2**, as the consequences are not so dire, the number tested will be lower and the conditions less stringent.

Examples   Look at our five examples (A–E) and think about the penalties for making the two sorts of error.

To continue our example:

- *Type I error*: Concluding that heated driving seats are dangerous when in fact they are not. The consequences would be that the motoring public are deprived of a popular accessory.
- *Type II error*: Concluding that heated driving seats make no difference to the accident rate when in fact they do. If in fact the accident rate is higher, dangerous accessories are being allowed onto the market.

ONE- AND TWO-TAILED TESTS

Suppose our testing is designed to show whether or not an unknown μ has a certain value μ_0. The null-hypothesis H_0 is that it does have this value, the alternative hypothesis H_1 is that it does not. There are two sorts of alternative hypotheses to be distinguished.

Unless there is reason to suppose otherwise, the alternative hypothesis is simply that μ is different from μ_0. In symbols, we write:

$$H_1 : \mu \neq \mu_0$$

This is called a *two-tailed* test. The value of μ could be either greater than μ_0 or less than it. There are many circumstances in which μ could only be greater than μ_0 (or only less than it) and these are called *one-tailed* tests. In these cases the alternative hypothesis will be written:

$$H_1 : \mu > \mu_0 \quad (\text{or as } H_1 : \mu < \mu_0)$$

Suppose we conduct a test to see whether or not consumption of a small amount of alcohol has an effect on manual dexterity. We would ask a group of people to perform some task, first sober and then after consuming two glasses of wine. The scores before and after would be compared.

The null hypothesis would be that manual dexterity is not changed by this amount of alcohol. The alternative hypothesis is that it *is* changed. But dexterity can only get worse after drinking wine, and so the alternative hypotheses would be one-tailed. H_1 would be that the expected score after drinking is lower than before.

We have already seen another example of a one-tailed test. The manufacturer of climbing ropes is only concerned if the breaking strength of the ropes is too low. It does not matter, in fact it is all to the good, if it is higher than claimed. So the test of the ropes' breaking strength is one-tailed.

A few points to note here. If we do a one-tailed test, then this must be decided *before* the test is carried out. It is not valid to look at the results and then decide that a one-tailed test is appropriate. We must have reason to suppose that the results could only go one way, or only be interested if the results go one way.

It is not always obvious whether a one- or a two-tailed test is appropriate. In the dexterity example above, a determined drinker could perhaps claim that a couple of glasses improved his dexterity.

The distinction between one- and two-tailed tests does not apply to all tests. Suppose we are testing to see whether there is a connection between the political party people support and the amount of television they view per week. The null hypothesis for this test will be that there is no connection between party supported and number of hours of TV viewing, that for example the supporters of Party A are just as likely to view over 20 hours a week as the supporters of Party B or Party C. There are many ways that this null hypothesis could be false: Party A's supporters might be more likely to view over 20 hours, Party B's supporters might be more likely to view less than 2 hours, and so on. The alternative hypothesis cannot be split up into two simple cases of $\mu > \mu_0$ or $\mu < \mu_0$.

Examples   Now look at our five running examples (A–E) and see whether they can be classified as one-tailed or two-tailed or neither. We shall do the first example, which involved the fitting of heated driving seats to cars. Did this affect the accident rate?

There is no prior reason to think that the rate will become greater or less with these accessories. If the driver is warm and comfortable, then one could argue that he is free to concentrate on driving. But one could also argue that he becomes more likely to fall asleep at the wheel. There are reasonable arguments for both sides, so the test should be two-tailed.

CONCLUSIONS FROM TESTS

The basic principles of null and alternative hypotheses, Type I and Type II errors are common to all tests. What varies are the arithmetical calculations that you make and the statistical tables in which you look up figures.

In the next chapter, we shall look at our five examples, giving numerical data for each of them, and seeing what statistical conclusions can be drawn.

6   Tests

In Chapter 5, we discussed the statistical basis of drawing conclusions from data. We gave five examples of situations in which conclusions might be drawn. Here we suppose that the data have been collected, by a survey of some sort, and we shall do the calculations from which results can be obtained.

The mathematics involved in statistics is very complicated. We shall not attempt to show how the formulas concerned are derived. We shall just present them, and show you how they are to be used in practical situations. Statistics is used by people in other disciplines as a tool – they do not have to know how the tools were constructed. After all, people can use a computer with confidence without knowing the details of its circuitry.

TESTS

Certain elements are common to most statistical tests. There is the null hypothesis H_0, and the alternative hypothesis H_1. There is the level of significance, which depends on the circumstances of the test. These were defined in the previous chapter. Here we shall use an example to remind you of these elements. Suppose there is a street intersection at which there is a very high rate of accidents, called a 'Black Spot'. Let us suppose that over a long period the average rate of accidents is 5 per month, with standard deviation 2. (Recall that the standard deviation is a measure of the dispersion of the data.) The local authorities put up warning signs on the streets leading to the Black Spot.

The null hypothesis is that the warning signs have made no difference to the rate of accidents. The alternative hypothesis is that they have decreased the rate.

Suppose the experiment or survey has been done. We will have collected a mass of data. In the Black Spot example, the rate of accidents is monitored for the next 12 months.We summarize the results by a single number, which is obtained by some function from the data. For example, we can summarize a collection of numbers by its average. In the Black Spot example, the average monthly rate will be found.

In every test, we start by assuming the null hypothesis H_0. Suppose that we found that over the 12 months the average rate of accidents was 3. Associated with this result there will be a probability. This is the probability of obtaining a result as different as this is from the expected result. The associated probability is the probability of obtaining 3 or fewer accidents per month, given that the true rate is still 5. The calculations will show that this probability is very low, about 0.0003. But if we had found that the average over the 12 months had been 4.8, not much less than 5, the associated probability would have been quite large, about 0.4.

The significance level of the test is the probability at which the test is said to be effective. For the Black Spot example, it will be the probability for which the authorities decide that the signs have been effective, and put up similar signs in other Black Spots. The level of significance will depend on the cost of the signs and the efficacy of other measures. Perhaps the level of significance is set at 5%.

If the associated probability is less than the significance level of the test, we will have disproved H_0 and proved H_1, at this significance level. This means that the hypothesis that the warning signs have made no difference to the accident rate cannot be sustained. Instead, we have the alternative hypothesis, which is that the signs have made a difference to the accident rate. Of course, as we took pains to point out in the previous chapter, we will not have proved the result with certainty.

If the probability is greater than the significance level, then we retain H_0. Again, note that we have not *proved* H_0. We have merely failed to *disprove* it.

For the Black Spot example, the probability associated with an average rate of 3 is much less than 5%. So we will have *dis*proved the null hypothesis, and signs will be introduced forthwith. The probability associated with an average rate of 4.8 is greater than 5%. We have not disproved H_0, and the authorities will look for other ways of reducing the accident rate.

So often the procedure is to apply a function to the data. The function, whatever it is, is called the *test statistic*. We then see whether or not the test statistic is above or below a fixed value. If it is above, then the associated probability is less than the significance level, and so we will have disproved H_0 at this significance level. In this case, we need not find the exact probability, as we know that it is less than 5%.

Normal distribution

There is one distribution which stands out from the rest in importance. This is called the *normal* distribution, which is illustrated by the bell-shaped curve shown in Fig. 6.1. In very many cases, the test statistic is such that it comes from the normal distribution, or approximately so. Let us suppose we are doing a test with a significance level of 5%. The shaded part of Fig. 6.1 comprises 5% of the total area, so that if our test statistic is in this region,

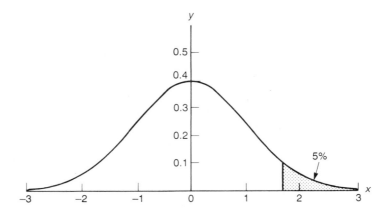

Figure 6.1

the associated probability is less than 5%. For a normal distribution with mean 0 and variance 1, the cut-off point for this is 1.64.

The distribution illustrated is called the *standard* normal distribution, in which the mean is 0 and the variance 1. As the normal distribution occurs so often, there is a special notation for it. If a normal distribution has mean μ and variance σ^2, we say it is $N(\mu, \sigma^2)$. The standard normal distribution is $N(0, 1)$. In general, the cut-off point for 5% of probability is 1.64σ (1.64 standard deviations) away from the mean.

One- and two-tailed tests

In Chapter 5, we made a distinction between one- and two-tailed tests. If the null hypothesis could only be wrong in one direction, or if we are only concerned if it goes wrong in one direction, then we do a one-tailed test. If it could go wrong in two directions, we do a two-tailed test. In the accident example, the new warning signs can only *lessen* the accident rate. So we do a one-tailed test.

With a one-tailed test, we look at only one end of the normal curve. With a two-tailed test, we look at both ends. For a 5% test, we will have 2.5% of probability at each end, as shown in Fig. 6.2. There is a higher cut-off point for 2.5% than for 5%. For the standard normal distribution $N(0, 1)$, it is 1.96 as opposed to 1.64.

So if we are testing at 5% significance, we use the 1.64 figure for a one-tailed test, and the 1.96 figure for a two-tailed test.

Having discussed the features which are common to all tests, we are ready to apply them to our particular examples.

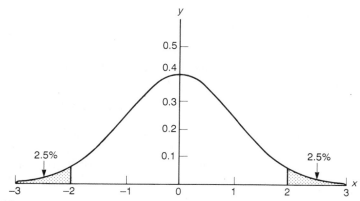

Figure 6.2

TESTS ON MEAN: EXAMPLE A

Example **A** in the previous chapter involved heated driving seats for cars. We supposed that Amalgamated Motors provided this accessory for its Siesta range. A motoring organization expressed concern about the safety aspects.

We shall express the safety of the cars in terms of insurance claims. Suppose that the average annual claim made by Siesta drivers is £100, with standard deviation £50. When the sample of 1000 cars with heated seats was made, it was found that the average claim was £105. Is this significantly different from £100?

The null hypothesis is that the heated seats do not alter the accident rate. The alternative hypothesis is that they do. Note that we are not assuming that the alteration goes in one direction rather than the other, so we shall perform a two-tailed test. Let us assign a symbol to the thing we are investigating. Let the mean insurance claim for cars with these seats be £μ. This mean μ is the mean for all cars with the seats. Be careful to distinguish this mean from the mean of the 1000 cars we have investigated.

Now we can state our null and alternative hypotheses:

$$H_0 : \mu = 100 \qquad \text{The mean is 100}$$
$$H_1 : \mu \neq 100 \qquad \text{The mean is not equal to 100}$$

We investigated a sample of n cars (in this case $n = 1000$) and found an average of £$\bar{x}$ (in this case $\bar{x}$ is £105). We want our test to measure the difference between the sample mean $\bar{x}$ and the expected population mean μ. It must also take account of the size of the sample, and the standard deviation of the population. By mathematical calculations, which we shall not put in here, the test statistic is:

$$z = \frac{\bar{x} - \mu}{\sqrt{\sigma^2/n}}$$

So to derive z, the population mean is subtracted from the sample mean. The result is then divided by the square root of the standard deviation of the population divided by the number of the sample:

$$n = 1000 \quad \mu = 100 \quad \bar{x} = 105 \quad \sigma^2 = 50^2 = 2500$$

$$z = \frac{105 - 100}{\sqrt{2500/1000}} = 3.16$$

It is difficult to give a direct interpretation of z. It is a standardized measure, to tell us how different the test results are from what we expect.

Assuming the null hypothesis, the distribution of z is normal with mean 0 and variance 1. In fact, we found a value of 3.16. What is the probability of finding a value as different from 0 as this?

The cut-off point for 2.5% of probability is 1.96, as shown in Fig. 6.2. If the null hypothesis were true, then we would have a probability of 5% of obtaining a z-value greater than 1.96. The value we have obtained is greater than this, so that the probability of obtaining a score as different from 0 as 3.16 is less that 5%. At the 5% level of significance, we have disproved the null hypothesis. We can now state our conclusion:

At a 5% level of significance, we have shown that there is a connection between the heated seats and the accident rate.

Exercises

(a) The average height for the adult male population is 1.8 m with a standard deviation of 0.1 m. Out of a sample of 80 smokers, the average height was found to be 1.78 m. Is the difference between the population average height and that of the sample significant? Calculate the value of z and work out whether it is significant at the 5% level.

(b) The mean recovery rate for gallstone operations in 20 private hospitals is 90%, while that in all hospitals is 88% with a standard deviation of 8%. Are the private hospitals significantly more effective than all the hospitals in the state taken as a whole?

TESTS ON CORRELATION: EXAMPLE B

Example **B** of the previous chapter involved a teacher who was trying to show that there is a connection between the hours of study per week and the mark in the end-of-year exam. Let us suppose the survey is done. The teacher questioned 20 children about how many hours per week they spent studying. The results we shall call x. The exam results were found at the end of the year, and these we shall call y. So, for example, if the 17th child studied for 7 hours per week and obtained 48% in the final exam, then $x_{17} = 7$ and $y_{17} = 48$.

There is a measure of how closely two quantities are connected, called the *correlation coefficient*. The formula was defined in Chapter 4. The correlation coefficient between x and y is given by the formula:

$$r = \frac{\Sigma xy/n - \bar{x}\bar{y}}{\sqrt{(\Sigma x^2/n - \bar{x}^2)(\Sigma y^2/n - \bar{y})}}$$

Here $\bar{x}$ and $\bar{y}$ refer to the means of the x- and y-values. Σx^2 refers to the sum of the squares of all the x-values.

To find Σxy, multiply together the pairs of values of x and y, and add them up. Suppose the results are given as in Table 6.1. We put in extra rows for x^2, y^2 and xy.

The sums we need for the correlation coefficient are:

$$\bar{x} = 3.55 \quad \bar{y} = 46.2 \quad \Sigma x^2 = 341 \quad \Sigma y^2 = 47{,}772 \quad \Sigma xy = 3480$$

Putting these into the formula for the correlation coefficient, we obtain:

$$r = \frac{3480/20 - 3.55 \times 46.2}{\sqrt{(341/20 - 3.55^2)(47772/20 - 46.2^2)}} = 0.297$$

We see that r is greater than zero. But is it significantly greater? Could this value have been obtained purely by chance? The way to find out is by using a statistical test.

There is a true correlation coefficient between the hours of study and the mark obtained, over all the children in the country. Call this ρ. Our null hypothesis is that there is no connection between the two factors:

$$H_0 : \rho = 0$$

The alternative hypothesis is that there is a connection. As extra study can only improve results, we do a one-tailed test:

$$H_1 : \rho > 0$$

Our test statistic is obtained by the formula:

$$z = r\sqrt{\left(\frac{n-2}{1-r^2}\right)}$$

Because we have a different situation, finding a correlation coefficient rather than a sample mean, the formula for finding the test statistic is different. But notice that both formulas have resulted in z, the variable from the standard normal distribution.

Table 6.1

x	6	5	4	6	2	4	1	7	0	2	5	3	4	1	0	2	7	4	3	5
y	32	44	51	39	38	45	53	69	78	31	58	47	59	18	17	29	48	63	40	65
x^2	36	25	16	36	4	16	1	49	0	4	25	9	16	1	0	4	49	16	9	25
y^2	1024	1936	2601	1521	1444	2025	2809	4761	6084	961	3364	2209	3481	324	289	841	2304	3969	1600	4225
xy	192	220	204	234	76	180	53	483	0	62	290	141	236	18	0	58	336	252	120	325

Here n is the number in the sample, in this case 20. r is the sample correlation coefficient, in this case $r = 0.297$. Evaluating this formula:

$$z = 1.32$$

Assuming the null hypothesis, the test statistic has a normal distribution with mean 0 and variance 1, i.e. it is $N(0, 1)$. The 5% cut-off value for this distribution is 1.64. Note that 1.32 is less than 1.64. This value of the correlation coefficient could have been obtained purely by chance, and we have not proved the alternative hypothesis. Note that we have not proved the null hypothesis, we have merely fa   disprove it. So our conclusions are:

At a 5% level of significance, we ha   proved that there is a connection between the time spent studying and   k obtained in the final exam.

Exercises

(a) Table 6.2 gives the average price (adjusted for inflation) of compact discs and the number purchased per year in a particular store. Find the correlation coefficient. Is it significantly different from zero at a 5% level? The year in which the data were collected does not affect the calculation.

Table 6.2   Number and price of compact discs sold, 1986–91

Year	No. of discs sold	Price (£)
1986	9,381	15.62
1987	10,237	14.39
1988	11,456	13.26
1989	12,937	12.95
1990	13,608	11.01
1991	15,097	10.08

(b) Table 6.3 shows the unemployment figures in percentages for a country and the number per 100,000 of deaths from stress-related diseases within the working population. Is the correlation significant? Once again, the year in which the data were obtained does not affect the calculation.

(c) Table 6.4 shows the emigration rates and crime rates for a European country in the nineteenth century. Emigration figures are the number of people actually leaving the country in that year, while the crime figures are those recorded by the Ministry for Public Order. Is there a significant association between the emigration figures and the rate of crime?

Table 6.3 Unemployment and death rates, 1980–87

Year	Rate of unemployment (%)	Death rate
1980	8.2	862
1981	8.5	876
1982	9.1	917
1983	9.3	902
1984	9.7	896
1985	10.2	1002
1986		1114
1987		1120

Table 6.4 Immigration and crime figures, 1820–24

Year	Immigration figures	Crime figures
1820	23,458	56,897
1821	36,129	52,963
1822	45,852	48,841
1823	60,093	45,542
1824	67,760	42,004

COMPARISON OF PROPORTION: EXAMPLE C

In Example **C** in the last chapter, a new medicine was tested: one group of 50 people was given the actual medicine, another group of 50 was given a placebo. None of the volunteers knew which group they were in. We then looked at the proportion in each group which claimed to feel better.

In the previous examples, a test result was compared with a fixed value – in **A** the test average was compared with the national average, and in **B** the test correlation was compared with zero. In this example, the results of two groups are compared with each other.

Let us suppose that the true proportions of people are π_1 and π_2 for the two groups. That is, if the medicine was administered to everybody with ME, then a proportion π_1 would report feeling better. If the placebo was administered to everybody, a proportion π_2 would report feeling better. Again note that the proportions π refer to the proportions in the population as a whole, not just to our small samples of 50. Our null hypothesis is that the medicine has no real effect, so that the two proportions are the same:

$$H_0 : \pi_1 = \pi_2$$
$$H_1 : \pi_1 > \pi_2$$

We do a one-tailed test here, as we assume that the medicine can only improve people's health.

Let us suppose that the sample proportions in the two groups are r_1 and r_2 respectively, and that the numbers in the groups are each n. We need to reduce the information we receive to a standard form that we can look up in tables. We need to reduce it to a variable from the normal distribution. This time we are testing difference of proportions. Our test statistic, which will have the standard normal distribution, is:

$$z = \frac{r_1 - r_2}{\sqrt{(r_1 + r_2)(1 - 1/2(r_1 + r_2))/n}}$$

In this situation $n = 50$. Let us suppose that the results of the experiment are:

- Of the group given the medicine, 35 reported feeling better.
- Of the group given the placebo, 28 reported feeling better.

Therefore:

$$r_1 = 35/50 = 0.7 \qquad r_2 = 28/50 = 0.56$$

So $z = 1.45$.

Assuming the null hypothesis, the test statistic z has a $N(0, 1)$ distribution. The 5% cut-off point for a one-tailed 5% test is 1.64, which is greater than 1.45. The test is inconclusive:

At a 5% significance level, there is no conclusive evidence that the medicine is effective.

Exercises
(a) A psychologist has carried out an experimental study of the effectiveness of assertiveness training in boosting confidence in demanding situations. She looks at two groups, each consisting of 100 women. Group A is given a course in assertiveness training and Group B is not. The members of both groups are then put into an experimental situation which involves displaying confidence.The experimenter compares the proportions rated 'very confident' in each group:

Group A   1 out of 4 very confident
Group B   1 out of 10 very confident

Is this significant at 5% to show that assertiveness training has had an effect on the confidence of the women?

(b) Some people think that owning a pet reduces stress. A dog food company sponsors research into dog ownership and stress patterns. Two groups are selected from the population, each consisting of 1000 adults. One group consists of dog owners, the other of people who do not own dogs. Each individual is given a questionnaire from which a 'stress index' is built up. The proportion of individuals in each group who cross the 'stress threshold' is then compared. The null hypothesis is that dog ownership makes no difference to stress patterns.

Proportion of dog owners crossing stress threshold   1 in 32
Proportion of non-dog owners crossing stress threshold   1 in 20

Is this significant at 5% to show that dog ownership affects stress levels?

NON-PARAMETRIC TESTS: EXAMPLE D

In many examples, we assume that the data come from a normal distribution. There are plenty of cases of data which do not come from this distribution; indeed, there are tests which do not make any assumptions about distributions at all. These are known as *non-parametric* or *distribution-free* tests.

Example **D** in the last chapter concerned the connection between tastes in music and social class. There is no natural way we can assign a number to a person's social class. If we pick a person at random, there is no distribution from which her social class comes. This is why we speak of the test we are about to perform as distribution-free. The best we can do is to arrange the people in order of class, without any assumptions about numerical values at all.

What we are measuring is whether the people in our sample like Waylon Anguish. In the list below, 30 people are ordered by social class. The letter underneath the number tells us whether that person likes or dislikes Waylon Anguish. Let L stand for liking, and D for disliking:

```
1   2   3   4   5   6   7   8   9   10  11  12  13  14  15  16  17
L   D   L   D   D   L   L   D   L   L   D   L   D   L   L   D   L
18  19  20  21  22  23  24  25  26  27  28  29  30
L   D   D   L   L   L   L   L   L   D   L   L   L
```

The people in our sample have been ranked according to social class using the Registrar General's classification according to socio-economic status, starting with people in class A (managerial and professional) on the left and ranging to E (unskilled) on the right.

Here we have 20 people who like Waylon Anguish and 10 who dislike him. What we look at is how the L's and D's are spread among the list. If there is a strong connection between class and liking, say that people from a higher socio-economic class tend to like him more than those from a lower class, then we would expect to see the L's at the front of the list and the D's at the end. If there is no connection, then we would expect to see the L's and D's scattered randomly throughout the list.

The people who dislike Waylon Anguish are ranked at 2, 4, 5, 8, 11, 13, 16, 19, 20 and 27. Add up these ranks to obtain $T = 125$. This total will be our measure of the randomness of the scattering. A large total would mean that the dislikers had large numbers for their ranks, and so were clustered nearer the bottom end of the social scale. A small total would mean that the dislikers had small numbers for their ranks, and so were clustered near the top end of the scale. How significant is a total of 125?

The null hypothesis is that there is no connection between class and liking. The alternative hypothesis is that there is a connection. Note that this is a two-tailed test – we do not have any assumptions about whether Waylon Anguish is more popular among those people of a higher or a lower socio-economic class. Note also that we are not giving a numerical value to our hypotheses, as this is a non-parametric test.

To find the significance of the result, again we convert it to a normal distribution. If the null hypothesis H_0 is true, i.e. if there is no connection between class and taste, then the total T will be approximately normally distributed.

Although the situation is not numerical, we can represent the results numerically. We can convert the result to the standard normal distribution by the following test statistic:

$$z = \frac{T - n_1(n_1 + n_2 + 1)/2}{\sqrt{n_1 n_2 (n_1 + n_2 + 1)/12}}$$

(Here n_1 and n_2 refer to the number of people who dislike and like Waylon Anguish, respectively.)

For our figures, $n_1 = 10$, $n_2 = 20$, $T = 125$. Put these into the formula and we obtain $z = 1.32$. This is less than 1.96, the cut-off point for a significance level of 5%. We have not proved the alternative hypothesis, and we retain the null hypothesis:

At a 5% level of significance, we have not shown that there is a connection between income and taste in music.

Exercises   (a) Below is given the order of finishing in a 'fun run' for charity. Some of the participants practised beforehand (P) and others did not (N). Is there an association between practice beforehand and performance in the run?

1st	2nd	3rd	4th	5th	6th	7th	8th	9th	10th	11th	12th	13th	14th	15th
P	P	N	N	P	P	P	N	P	N	P	N	N	N	N

(b) The hierarchy of employment within an organization is expressed on a 14 point scale, ranging from 1 (managing director) to 14 (trainee storehand). Approval of innovation is indicated by A and disapproval by D. This designation is arrived at by looking at whether or not a majority of employees in each category expressed approval or disapproval and then registering the majority result.

1	2	3	4	5	6	7	8	9	10	11	12	13	14
A	A	D	A	D	D	A	A	D	D	A	D	D	D

Is this significant at 5% to show there is a connection between approval and position in the organization's hierarchy?

CONTINGENCY TABLES: EXAMPLE E

Example **E** in the previous chapter introduced the effects of different methods of teaching children how to read. Let us suppose there are three methods in common use, called Phonics, Look and Say (L&S) and Language Experience (LE). Let us suppose that 200 children who have been taught by these methods are tested at eight, and are classified according to whether their reading ability is good, medium or bad. The results might be as given as in Table 6.5. These are called the *observed* frequencies. Notice we also provide the row and column totals.

Table 6.5 Children's reading ability by method of teaching: Observed frequencies

	Phonics	*L&S*	*LE*	*Total*
Good	15	21	34	70
Medium	32	24	12	68
Bad	38	14	10	62
Total	85	59	56	200

Do these results show that any of the methods is significantly better than the others? We are testing more things here than in the previous examples, as there are three sorts of method and three classifications of result. It does not make sense to speak of a one-tailed or two-tailed test here.

Again the null hypothesis is that there is no connection between teaching method and result. The alternative hypothesis is that there is a connection. If we assume the null hypothesis, then the proportions of good, medium and bad readers should be the same for all three methods.

For example, the proportion of good readers overall is $\frac{70}{200} = 0.35$. The proportion of medium readers overall is $\frac{68}{200} = 0.34$, and the proportion of bad readers is $\frac{62}{200} = 0.31$. Within each method column the proportions of good, medium and bad readers should be the same. Take the first column, of the 85 children taught by the Phonics method, 35% should be good readers, 34% medium and 31% bad.

We can work out these proportions:

35% of 85 is 29.75
34% of 85 is 28.9
31% of 85 is 26.35

We now put these figures into the first column of a new table. And so on. The entry in each box can be quickly found by multiplying together the row total and the column total and then dividing by 200. The new table is shown as Table 6.6. These are called the *expected* frequencies.

Table 6.6 Children's reading ability by method of teaching: Expected frequencies

	Phonics	*L&S*	*LE*	*Total*
Good	29.75	20.65	19.6	70
Medium	28.9	20.06	19.04	68
Bad	26.35	18.29	17.36	62
Total	85	59	56	200

We now compare the observed frequencies with the expected ones. If the null hypothesis is true, i.e. all the teaching methods are equally effective, then there should not be much difference between Tables 6.5 and 6.6. If there is a substantial difference, then that means that one method is likely to be superior to the others. The test statistic to measure the difference between the tables is:

$$\chi^2 = \Sigma (f_e - f_o)^2 / f_e$$

where f_e stands for the expected frequencies and f_o for the observed frequencies.

The actual derivation of this formula is complicated. But notice that the $(f_e - f_o)^2$ terms measure the difference between the expected and observed frequencies. We divide each of these by the corresponding f_e, in order to measure the difference as a proportion of the expected frequency. In our case, this comes to:

$$\chi^2 = (29.75 - 15)^2 / 29.75 + (20.65 - 21)^2 / 20.65 + \cdots + (17.36 - 10)^2 / 17.36$$

So for each box we subtract the observed frequency from the expected, square this figure, then divide by the expected frequency. This is a good exercise in the use of a calculator.

The result is 30.88. Is this significantly large? Again we refer to tables, in this case for the χ^2 function (see Table 6.7).

Table 6.7   Critical values of the χ^2 distribution

Degrees of freedom	10%	5%	1%	0.1%
$v = 1$	2.71	3.84	6.63	10.83
$v = 2$	4.61	5.99	9.21	13.81
$v = 3$	6.25	7.81	11.34	16.27
$v = 4$	7.78	9.49	13.28	18.47
$v = 5$	9.24	11.07	15.09	20.52
$v = 6$	10.64	12.59	16.81	22.46

The phrase 'degrees of freedom' is linked to the number of boxes we are comparing. Our tables contain nine boxes each. But when we constructed the expected frequencies in Table 6.6, we did not have nine free choices for what to put in the boxes. We had to ensure that the row and column totals were the same for both tables. So the bottom row and the right column were determined by the totals: we have only $(3 - 1) \times (3 - 1) = 4$ free entries in the table. In general, if a table has n rows and m columns, the number of degrees of freedom is $(n - 1) \times (m - 1)$.

This is a χ^2 test with 4 degrees of freedom. The 5% cut-off point for this test is 9.49, considerably less than 30.88. We do have a significant result. Our conclusion is:

At a 5% significance level, we have shown there is a connection between teaching method and ability to read.

Exercises

(a) Table 6.8 lists the results of different experimental treatments for a common chronic disease. Recovery in this case means remission from symptoms for more than one year. Do these figures show there is a significant difference in the efficacy of the different treatments?

Table 6.8   Recovery rates by treatment

	Oxygen chamber	Drugs	Special diet	No treatment
Recovery	40	25	10	30
No recovery	10	25	40	20

(b) A school board is trying to find the best way to eliminate bullying in its schools. Various proposals are tested. Success is measured by a 50%

drop in reported cases of bullying. Do these figures show a significant difference in the efficacy of these methods?

Table 6.9   Success at reducing bullying

	Counselling	Confrontation with victim	Suspension
Successful	10	15	30
Not successful	20	15	10

(c) A survey of 500 doctors was carried out to find how their religion affected their occupation. The results are given in Table 6.10. Are these results significant at 5% to show there is a connection between religion and occupation?

Table 6.10   The effects of religion on occupation

	Christian	Muslim	Other religion	No religion
General practitioner	100	30	40	180
Consultant	20	5	10	15
Registrars	30	20	20	30

CONFIDENCE INTERVALS

In the five tests above, we were testing a hypothesis against the data which had been collected. Sometimes we have no preconceived ideas at all, and that all we know about the situation is derived from the data. For example, if we spin a bent coin, we will have no prior idea what probability there is that it will land heads upwards. The only way to find out is by repeated experiment.

Suppose we toss the coin 100 times and obtain 30 heads. We are not certain that the true probability is 0.3. We can, however, give an interval, perhaps 0.29 to 0.31, which we are fairly confident contains the true probability. This interval is called a *confidence interval*.

Let us take, for example, the situation of Example **A**, which involved the insurance claims of certain motorists. Suppose we have no prior idea of what the true mean is, and that we have to find it from the data. A 95% confidence interval will be one which contains the true mean with probability 0.95.

The test we did was to determine whether or not the average claim of these motorists was £100. The test statistic we used was:

$$\frac{\bar{x} - \mu}{\dfrac{\sigma}{\sqrt{1000}}}$$

We use a function very similar to this test statistic. The denominator of the expression above is the standard deviation of the difference from the mean. It was put in to standardize the test statistic by giving it a standard deviation of 1, so that it would come from the N(0,1) distribution.

Recall that the cut-off figure for the N(0,1) distribution, at a significance level of 5%, is 1.96. Values greater than this can only come about with probability less than 0.05. So we bring this into our confidence interval also. We are 95% confident that the normal z will not be more than 1.96 away from 0. So we will be 95% confident that the true mean will not be more than $1.96 \times \sigma/\sqrt{1000}$ away from the observed mean.

Figure 6.3 shows the observed mean, and two normal curves on either side of it. With probability 0.95, the interval between the two peaks of the curves will contain the true mean μ.

Figure 6.3

The confidence interval for the true mean will be 1.96 times the standard deviation on either side of the observed mean. So if the observed mean is x, the confidence interval for μ will be:

$$\bar{x} - \frac{1.96\sigma}{\sqrt{1000}} \quad \text{to} \quad \bar{x} + \frac{1.96\sigma}{\sqrt{1000}}$$

Now let us look at our figures. The sample mean of 1000 observations was 105. The interval which contains the mean with probability 0.95 is:

$$105 - \frac{1.96\sigma}{\sqrt{1000}} < \mu < 105 + \frac{1.96\sigma}{\sqrt{1000}}$$

Here the standard deviation σ is 50. Our confidence interval is:

$$102 < \mu < 108$$

Notice that the variation on either side of the sample mean is divided by the square root of the size of the sample. If we take a larger sample, then the variation of the sample will decrease, as we are dividing the standard deviation by a larger number. We will be able to make the confidence interval narrower. But obtaining a larger sample may be expensive. As so often in statistics, the researcher has to make a decision about how much investigation can be afforded to obtain results which will give useful information.

Exercises (a) A new exam is piloted by being taken by 100 randomly selected schoolchildren. The average score was 52%, with a standard deviation of 11%. Find a 95% confidence interval for the mean score when the exam is taken by all the children in the country.

(b) A survey into the drinking habits of the population of a city measured the alcohol consumption of 200 people. They were found to consume an average of 30 units per week, with standard deviation 10 units. Find a 95% confidence interval for the mean weekly consumption of the population as a whole.

PART TWO
Computing

7   Hardware

The jargon words associated with computers have been steadily infiltrating our lives for many years. Anyone starting to use computers has to learn them, because they are necessary to describe the structure and capabilities of computer technology. Words like 'WYSIWYG' and 'megabyte' may be thought unlovely, but they summarize ideas which would take long to explain in ordinary English. Two words which are central to the understanding of computers are *hardware* and *software*.

- *Hardware* is the actual machinery of the computer. It consists of all the solid things which can be seen and felt. The monitor (the thing which looks like a television), the keyboard and the printer are all items of hardware.
- *Software* comprises the programs which the computer obeys. It consists of instructions and information, written down or recorded on disks or tapes. It is no more solid than a poem or piece of music.

An analogy with music might be helpful here. The hardware of music consists of the instruments on which it is made and the record-players or cassette-recorders which play it. The software of music consists of the tunes which the hardware can play.

Hardware and software are useless without each other. Again, this follows the musical analogy. There is no point in owning compact discs, if you have no compact disc player. There is no point in buying a piano, if you are incapable of ever playing any music on it.

In this chapter, we shall be talking about hardware, particularly that of microcomputers. The next chapter will be devoted to software.

THE EVOLUTION OF COMPUTERS

What should be called the first computer? This is a matter for debate and national pride. Calculating machines were built in the seventeenth century, but their functions were limited to the basic operations of adding, subtracting, multiplying and dividing. A characteristic of a computer is that it is capable of many different tasks, and can remember and obey a set of instructions (i.e. a program) to do these tasks.

In the nineteenth century, the English mathematician Charles Babbage devised such a machine. He called it the Analytic Engine, and it would have been able to perform a wide variety of calculating tasks. Punched cards would be fed into the machine to tell it which task to do. The numbers on which the machine would act would also be fed in on punched cards.

Unfortunately, the machine was never built. Even if it had been made, it would not have functioned reliably. The machine would have been powered by steam, and the calculation would have been done by cog wheels and rods. There would have been hundreds of moving parts, and it would have been continually breaking down.

Babbage's ideas about mechanical calculating were sound, even if nineteenth-century technology was not advanced enough to put them into practice. Practicable computers had to wait until the invention of electronics, which allowed for the construction of devices in which there are no moving parts to break down or wear out. One could say that Babbage's notions of software were adequate, but that Victorian engineering could not provide satisfactory hardware.

The Analytic Engine would have recorded numbers in the ordinary, decimal way, using the ten digits 0 up to 9. But modern computers use an arithmetic based on only two digits, 0 and 1. The reasons are as follows.

The electronic components that make up a computer can be in either of two states. They can be *on* or *off*. So we let the *on* state represent the number 1, and the *off* state represent 0. From this very simple representation any number can be built up, as a succession of 0's and 1's. The system of rules which these numbers obey is called *binary arithmetic*. All the calculation of computers, involving vast quantities of figures, is done by manipulating huge numbers of 0's and 1's.

The first electronic computers were developed in Britain and the USA in the 1940s. Very many of the features of the early computers, in particular the use of binary arithmetic, are still in evidence. The basic logical structure devised in the 1940s is still the foundation of most modern computers.

The most striking changes have been in the physical equipment with which the computer carries out its tasks, that is in the hardware of the computer. It is often said that there are four generations of computers, and that we are on the eve of the fifth.

GENERATIONS OF COMPUTERS

- *First-generation computers.* The computer originally used thermionic valves (things which look a bit like lightbulbs) for its work. Pulses of electricity which represented numbers in binary notation passed through the valves, resulting in an 'answer' at the end of the operation. This answer was also a sequence of pulses, representing a binary number. Old-fashioned radios used valves, and if you have ever used one you may remember how hot it can get. Early computers, using thousands of valves, could get very hot indeed.

● *Second-generation computers.* Transistors were used for the second generation. They can perform all the functions of valves, but faster and using much less electrical power. The second generation began in the 1950s.

● *Third-generation computers.* The transistors of the second generation were joined by a maze of wires. For the third generation, beginning in the 1960s, several electronic components were combined on a single piece of silicon, called a *chip.*

● *Fourth-generation computers.* Gradually it became possible to put more and more components on a chip. Fourth-generation computers use chips which have thousands of components packed onto a small space, a technique called Very Large Scale Integration (VLSI). So nowadays it is the chip of the computer which does all the work, of deciding which arithmetic operation to do and then doing it.

COMPUTER DEVELOPMENT

The hardware of computers has evolved through these four generations, roughly one per decade. This evolution has brought about several quite breathtaking changes in the impact computers have on our lives.

● *Decrease in size.* One early computer was called ENIAC (Electronic Numerical Integrator And Computer). It weighed about 50 tons and occupied a huge area. Today there are 'laptop' computers, about the size of a handbag, which are much more powerful in computing terms than ENIAC.

● *Decrease in cost.* Computers were first used commercially in the 1950s, and they cost millions of pounds or dollars. A modern computer which could perform the same tasks might cost a few hundred pounds or dollars.

● *Increase in power.* The electronic technology has increased at such a rate that what ENIAC took 24 hours to do can now be done in a few seconds.

● *Variety of applications.* The early computers of the 1940s were used for narrowly defined, highly mathematical purposes. One vital use was in code-breaking during the Second World War. Nowadays computers are used in a spectrum of activities ranging from controlling a space rocket to playing Space Invaders.

● *Increase of ownership.* In their early days, computers were owned by universities, large companies and governments. Now they are commonplace items of household equipment.

None of these spectacular developments was foreseen. The British mathematician Alan Turing, one of the inventors of the computer, predicted that four or five computers would be adequate to do all the computing business for the whole world. He underestimated by a factor of many million! Indeed, a consistent feature of the short history of computers has been the way in which their importance and capabilities have been underestimated. It may be that in ten years time, we will look back and realize how much we now underestimate the computer.

MAINFRAMES, MINIS, MICROS

- *Mainframes*. There are still computers which are large and expensive. They are used by large institutions for big tasks, such as handling the ticket sales of a major airline or calculating the tax payable for the citizens of a state. These are called *mainframe* computers. There will be several terminals for a mainframe computer, so that several people can use it at the same time. A bank, for example, will use a mainframe computer for all its calculations. There will be terminals in all the branches of the bank, so that a customer can enter any of the branches and withdraw or deposit money in his or her account.
- *Minis*. Nowadays it is common for the mainframe to be replaced by a network of mid-sized computers, sometimes called 'minis', which share the jobs between themselves.
- *Micros*. The small computers which can be bought by ordinary people are called *microcomputers*. Because they have become so much more powerful, they are used by firms which previously might have hired time on a mainframe computer.
- *LANs*. This stands for Local Area Network. An office or a university department might have several computers linked together by a network. The computers can communicate with each other. In particular, there is a central computer called the *server*, which can provide information to the other computers, called *clients*.

MICROCOMPUTERS

The sort of computer you are most likely to own or have direct experience of is a microcomputer. We shall concentrate on these for the rest of the chapter.

Figure 7.1 shows a photo of a microcomputer. This is the hardware, and it has several components.

A   *The systems unit*. The actual computer is inside the rectangular box. Recall that the chip is the item which does all the operations of calculation

Figure 7.1

and control: the chip is inside here, and it is very unlikely that you would ever have to dig it out.

B *The keyboard*. This is like a typewriter keyboard, though with many more keys. From here you can type in your instructions, which are then sent to the computer.

C *The monitor*. Also called the Visual Display Unit (VDU). This is like a television. In fact, some inexpensive computers can use an ordinary television as their monitor. The monitor shows information to tell the user what is happening inside the computer. Some monitors are mono (black and white) others are in colour.

D *The printer*. Any information shown on the monitor will disappear once it is switched off. If you want a permanent record of your work, you can print it out on the printer.

E *The mouse*. This provides another way of giving instructions to your computer, instead of typing them in at the keyboard. The mouse can be moved around to control a pointer on the monitor screen, and buttons on the mouse can be pressed to perform certain tasks. This small object, with a tail that connects it to the computer, looks enough like a small rodent for computer experts to call it a 'mouse'.

So to summarize, there is the systems unit which does all the work, and there are the devices which convey information to and from the unit. These are either input or output devices:

- *Input*: the keyboard and the mouse send information to the computer.
- *Output*: the monitor and the printer take information from the computer. The monitor shows it on the screen, and the printer puts it on paper.

There are other input and output devices. One is the modem, which works both ways. It connects the computer to the telephone system, so that your computer can either send information to other computers or receive information from them. If the computer is part of a network, it will be connected to a cable through which it can share information with the other computers on the network.

Disks

Another very important way of getting information to and from the computer is by *disks*. At the front of the system unit **A** there are one or more slots called disk-drives. Disks are inserted into these slots, and information can be transmitted from the disk to the computer. Going the other way, the computer can put information on the disk, which can then be taken out and, for example, used in another computer. As they are so important, we shall be dealing with disks in a separate section.

MEMORY

Computers generate and use a vast quantity of information. Part of their usefulness is that they can handle amounts of figures or facts which would occupy armies of clerks. Just think of the labour involved in working out the income tax for every adult in a state! At a more humble level, you might use a computer to write a thesis or novel. This involves hundreds of thousands of letters. The computer must somehow memorize and store all the information it is given.

Bytes, kilobytes, megabytes, gigabytes, terabytes

In practice, the smallest unit that the computer handles is the *byte*. Recall that a computer deals with components which can be in one of two states, representing either 0 or 1. A group of eight of these components makes up a byte. Each of these components can be either 0 or 1, so the byte itself can represent $2 \times 2 \times 2 \times 2 \times 2 \times 2 \times 2 \times 2 = 256$ different numbers. For example, the string 01000001 represents the number 65. The following demonstrates how 65 is represented in binary:

128 64 32 16 8 4 2 1
  0   1   0   0 0 0 0 1   so 0100001 represents $64 + 1 = 65$

So each byte records one number. This number may represent an actual number if the computer is doing numerical work, or it may represent a letter if the computer is handling text. If you are writing a thesis on a computer, it will be remembered as a string of numbers, each of which occupies a byte of memory, and each of which represents a letter. Under one standard code, the number 65 represents capital A.

A *kilobyte* (kB) is a thousand bytes, just as a kilometre is a thousand metres. (In fact, because the computer works in powers of 2, it is $2^{10} = 1024$ bytes.) So a kilobyte of memory will store a short paragraph.

A *megabyte* is a thousand kilobytes, i.e. a million bytes (strictly, $2^{20} = $ 1,048,576 bytes). A megabyte of memory is enough to store a typical novel.

A *gigabyte* is a thousand megabytes, and a *terabyte* is a thousand gigabytes. A whole library could be stored on a terabyte.

All this memory is kept in different ways.

RAM

Inside the systems unit is RAM (Random Access Memory). This is where the information is stored while the computer is in operation. If you are using a computer to write an article, what you have written so far will be stored in the RAM. Once the machine is switched off, though, all the things stored in the RAM are lost. So before you switch off, you must either print out your article or store it on another kind of memory.

Floppy disks

A way to store information so that it is not lost when the computer is switched off is by putting it on a floppy disk. These are disks coated with a magnetic material, on which information can be put. The disks themselves are floppy, but sometimes they are inside a firm plastic case. The disks can be inserted in the disk-drive of a computer, as mentioned above. They come in different sizes, and can store different amounts of material.

- $5\frac{1}{4}$ inch disks. These are $5\frac{1}{4}''$ in diameter, and are genuinely floppy. Normally they store either 360 or 720 kB of information.
- $3\frac{1}{2}$ inch disks. These are $3\frac{1}{2}''$ in diameter, and come in a hard plastic case. Normally they store either 720 or 1440 kB of information. Nowadays they are used much more frequently than the $5\frac{1}{4}''$ floppies.

So as a rough guide, one of these disks could be used to store a novel. A long novel could fit onto a $3\frac{1}{2}''$ disk with 1440 kB of memory, and a short one onto a $5\frac{1}{4}''$ disk with 320 kB. These disks are very cheap, and they can be transported between different computers.

Hard disks

Inside the systems unit of a computer there may be a hard disk. The differences between hard and floppy disks are as follows:

- The hard disk is expensive. It is a highly delicate piece of machinery.
- The hard disk can store much more information. A hard disc might have a capacity of between 30 MB and over 1000 MB. Even on a 30 MB hard disc, there is room to store 30 longish novels.
- The hard disk is fixed. Floppy disks can be taken in and out of the computer, and used in different computers. The hard disk remains inside one particular computer.

CD ROM

The information in RAM can be added to or altered. By contrast, ROM stands for Read Only Memory. The computer can take information from ROM, but not add to it or amend it in any way. A compact disk (CD) can be used to hold vast amounts of information. This is ROM information: with the aid of a device the computer can receive the information from the CD, but not transmit information to it.

PRINTERS

The output device that can be very expensive is the printer. You may require it to print out pictures as well as text. If you want to produce material that looks very good you will need a good printer, but if you just want something that gives a rough copy of your writing you can get by with a cheap one. There are several different types of printer available.

Dot-matrix

The print-head of a dot-matrix printer has a group of little pins which can be made to press against an inked ribbon on top of the paper. The computer can control which of the pins are pushed forward, and so can control which letter is printed. The disadvantage of these machines is that they are noisy and rather slow. They may take a few minutes to print a single page. The advantage is that they are cheap and robust. Two basic types are available.

- *9-pin*: As the name suggests, there are 9 pins on the print-head. This sort of printer is the cheapest available.
- *24-pin*: The head of this sort of printer has 24 pins, and so the quality of print is of a much higher standard. Another advantage is that it can be run in a manner called download mode, in which it can print any shape that the computer tells it to print. So if you need to print Greek or Cyrillic letters, you can do so on a 24-pin printer. Because the pins are finer, a 24-pin machine is more delicate than a 9-pin. In particular, a 24-pin printer is fussier about the sort of paper it will accept.

Ink-jet

This sort of printer squirts jets of ink at the paper to make the letters. This is a much less messy process than it sounds. The advantage of this sort of printer is that it is quiet and produces very high-quality print. However, they are more expensive than dot-matrix printers.

Laser

The best (and most expensive) sort of printers are called *laser* printers. Their operation is similar to that of a photocopier. They are expensive to run as well as to buy, as they need to be refilled with cartons of toner. But they are coming down in price, and are within the reach of the ordinary user. They are quiet and fast (about 4–12 pages per minute).

THE PERSONAL COMPUTER

There are very many firms which make computers. In terms of microcomputers, some important names are Apple Macintosh, Acorn, Toshiba, and so on. Apple Macintosh, in particular, played a very large role in extending the use of computers. But there is one company which stands out above the rest.

The market leader in the world of computers is IBM, known in the trade as 'Big Blue'. In the early 1980s, IBM produced the *personal computer* (PC). It was a microcomputer which was intended to be used by small businesses or educational institutions or even in the home. It became very successful.

A lot of software was written specially for the IBM personal computer. And then other computer manufacturers realized that they could tap into the market for microcomputers by following IBM.

Clones

A *clone* of the IBM microcomputer is a computer made by another company which can use all the software designed for IBM computers. They are said to be '*IBM-compatible*'. If they are described as being a 'PC', then they are IBM-compatible. Usually they are much cheaper than the IBM originals. Leaving aside those computers which are designed just for playing games, IBM-compatible computers (and those made by IBM itself) make up about 80% of the microcomputer market. Even in the leisure area, PCs are making headway. In 1992, Amstrad brought out a PC specifically designed for games-playing.

Recall that the heart of the computer is its chip, the thing that performs all the calculations. These chips have evolved, getting faster and more powerful. The speed of a chip is given in terms of megahertz (MHz). The greater the number, the faster the chip. (Though there are other factors which affect speed.) There has been a sequence of chips used in the PC, as follows:

8088 8086 80186 80286 80386 80486 80586 (also known as the 'Pentium')

This sequence seems likely to continue for many years. The chips have been gradually getting more powerful. When a PC is described in an advertisement, the number of its chip will be given, and when you buy a program you may find that it requires a computer with, for example, at least an 80286 chip in it.

The earlier chips in the sequence are no longer being made. They are said to be obsolete. Now, this does not mean that they can no longer be used. It just means that it will not be capable of handling the more advanced software that is being written. If all you want to do is basic word-processing, then an 8086-based computer is quite adequate. But to run other things such as desktop publishing (which we shall be mentioning in Chapter 9) or to play some of the more spectacular games, you need an 80286 or preferably an 80386. As software gets more complicated, you need better hardware to run it.

BUYING A COMPUTER

Why should I buy a computer?

It is much easier to learn about machines when one has to handle them oneself. And there is no greater incentive to learning quickly than having spent money on the machine. More and more people are realizing that their lives would be easier and more productive if they owned a computer, and are finding that they are less expensive than they thought.

You might be a student who up to now has typed out all your essays. At the end of the year, there might be a project which you will have to present, and the prospect of typing it out many times is very dispiriting. You know of the benefits of word-processing, and you might be considering buying a computer.

What should I buy?

There is a rule of thumb: 'Decide what software you want, then buy the hardware to run it'. If all you want to do is basic word-processing, then there are machines on the market which will do that and nothing else. The most basic form of PC (i.e. one with the earliest chip) will certainly be adequate for that. But there are drawbacks of which you should be aware:

- *Speed.* If you type a long document, an elementary computer will be very slow in going through it and printing it out.
- *Other uses.* At the moment you may think that word-processing is all you need. But you may realize that there are other things you could use your computer for, and it will be frustrating if your machine is not capable of them. In particular, if your project involves statistical diagrams, tables, illustrations, and so on, a simple word-processor will not be capable of handling them.

Portable or desktop?

Desktop computers look like the one illustrated on p. 105. They have more than one component, and it is quite an operation to move them around, even from one side of the room to the other. A portable computer can be quite small. Palmtop computers can be carried on one hand. Laptop computers are the size of a handbag. Because it costs money to make things small and robust, a portable computer is more expensive than the equivalent desktop. So unless you really have to work on planes and trains, you would be better off with a desktop.

When should I buy?

When is a good time to buy a computer? It is never a good time to buy a computer. Prices are going down even when allowances are made for inflation. Whenever you buy, a few months later you will have the galling experience of seeing the same equipment advertised at a considerably cheaper price. But if you refuse to buy a computer at all, then you will never enjoy the benefits of owning one.

Will it get out of date?

We have emphasized the rapid development of computers, so that what is the latest machine one year is on the way to becoming obsolete a couple of years later. It is understandable that you may feel reluctant to spend a lot of money on something that you may have to replace in a few years time. Computers are now made 'future-proof', so that they can be updated by the insertion of a new chip, or by the addition of extra memory, so it is unlikely that you will have to replace the whole machine.

What extras must I buy?

When a computer is advertised, it includes the systems unit and the monitor. It may also include a mouse and maybe some other items. It will not include a printer, and that is a major expense that you will have to think about.

If you just want a rough print-out of your work, then the cheapest dot-matrix printer will be adequate. You might be able to use another printer for when you want high-quality output. But if you regularly produce material that you want to look very good, then it is worth considering investing in a more expensive printer.

There are many other accessories that you can buy to go with your computer, but the computer itself, monitor and printer provide the essential hardware that you need.

How do I buy?

There are many ways you can buy a computer. Some high-street electrical shops sell computers, or can order them for you. There are specialist computer shops in big cities, and there are computer supermarkets with a very wide range of equipment available. You can also buy through mail order. There are many magazines devoted to computers, and they carry dozens of pages of advertisements. From these you can get a good idea of prices, as well as where to do your shopping. If you buy by mail order, it is wise to pay by credit card rather than cheque, as this provides a greater degree of consumer protection in the event of the firm going bankrupt before they deliver your goods.

STARTING UP

Let us assume that you have bought your equipment, from whatever source, and all the boxes are sitting on your floor. When you unpack, you would be wise to keep all the packaging material. If things go wrong and you have to send the machine back, they will require that it be sent in the original packaging.

You will follow the instructions about fixing plugs and connecting the various components together. You will switch it on to make sure that everything is working.

But there is nothing you can do with your computer until you have the software to run on it. And that is the subject of the next chapter.

8   Software

PROGRAMS

The previous chapter, on hardware, dealt with the actual solid machinery of a computer. Here we discuss the software, which converts a computer from a lump of metal and plastic to a machine capable of carrying out an enormous array of tasks with great speed and efficiency.

A *program* (the American spelling is standard) is a sequence of instructions which tell the computer what to do: one line of a program might tell the computer to add two numbers, the next line might tell it to print the result on the screen. At a commercial level, the job of writing programs is a highly specialized one, carried out by software firms. This book does not attempt to explain how to program a computer: we shall instead deal with the use of programs which have already been written. These are called *applications* programs.

Software consists of these programs, together with the information, in coded electronic form, on which the programs act.

An analogy we used in the previous chapter was that of music. The hardware of a computer is like a piano, and the software is like the tunes which can be played on the piano. Now, a piano can play any sort of music – it does not make much sense to say: 'This is a jazz piano'. The instrument can be classical, or jazz, or pop, depending on what music is being played on it. Modern computers can be used for many different purposes. It does not make much sense to say: 'This is a word-processing computer'. Computers are general-purpose machines: they can perform any task they are programmed to perform. The program that is loaded decides what the machine is doing, and can make it play a variety of different roles. Some are given in the next section.

TYPES OF SOFTWARE

The variety of programs has greatly increased over the past few years. More and more uses are being found for computers, as they become cheaper and more powerful. Below are some categories of software programs, along with a description of what they can make the computer do.

- *Games*. There are many games available for personal computers. With them loaded, the computer becomes a games-playing machine, like the ones in amusement arcades.
- *Word-processors*. A word-processor turns your computer into a super-typewriter. It can do a lot more than just writing text, though. You can correct your mistakes, move paragraphs from one place to another, and, with the more advanced programs, insert pictures and tables into anything you might be writing. We shall be considering this in more detail in Chapter 9.
- *Desk-top publishing*. With a desk-top publishing program, you can produce a page of a magazine, for example, which more or less looks exactly as you want it to. You can arrange the text in columns, and insert illustrations. These programs are like word-processors, but you have more control over how your pages are set out.
- *Spreadsheets*. A spreadsheet program turns your computer into a super-calculator. You can enter words and numbers, and perform a wide variety of calculations on them. The results you get can be shown in the form of a graph. Spreadsheets will be considered in Chapter 10.
- *Databases*. This sort of program turns your computer into a super-filing cabinet. You can keep records of people or items, and extract information from the records and make calculations based on them. These programs will be considered in Chapter 11.
- *Programming languages*. If you are writing a program, you must do so in a 'language' which the computer can understand. There are a great number of programming languages available. Some, like BASIC, are designed to be picked up quickly, and so are suitable for beginners. Others, like C, are more difficult but give the programmer more control over the computer.
- *Commercial software*. Many programs are written for businessmen and accountants, for example to help with budgeting or stock control.
- *Graphics*. These programs enable you to use a computer to create a picture. They can be used by designers.
- *Educational programs*. With this sort of program loaded, the computer can give you a lesson. For example, it could ask you to solve mathematical problems, or answer questions about geography.
- *Academic programs*. Specialized academic programs include statistical packages for social scientists and mathematical packages.
- *Utilities*. These are programs which help you to run your computer more efficiently and safely. For example, if the same picture shows on the screen for a long period, it is liable to etch itself permanently on the screen surface. There are utility programs called *screen savers* which cater for this. If the computer is left unattended for a few minutes, the contents of the screen will be removed and replaced by a moving pattern.

There are other classes of applications programs, and they are increasing as people find more and more uses for computers.

All these types of programs can be used on microcomputers, the sort of computer you are most likely to own and use. Large commercial and scientific computers can run other sorts of programs, which we shall not consider here.

BUYING SOFTWARE

Software is on sale in computer shops, and it can be bought by mail order. Computer magazines contain page after page of advertisements for software products, usually divided into the types of applications discussed in the previous section. Often when you buy a computer, it will come with one or more software packages, so you do not have to go and buy it separately.

What do you get in a software package? A program, consisting as it does of a set of instructions, is an abstract thing. But when you purchase software, you must buy something solid.

What you get is a box, or maybe a thick envelope. Figure 8.1 shows the box which contains a certain word-processing program. Inside the box will be a disk (or tape, for some programs). The actual program is on the disk or tape, coded in magnetic form. There will also be one or more books – usually a reference manual and a 'tutorial' helping you to use the program.

You can then put the disk into your machine, and either run the program directly from the disk or transfer its contents to your hard disk. Once the program is started, the tutorial will give you a sequence of lessons introducing you to what the program can do. The reference manual is usually more useful when you have already mastered the basics of the program, and need to remind yourself how to perform a particular task.

Versions

A software package, provided it is successful, will be regularly updated, rather as a successful book will be reprinted or have new editions. The new editions of a piece of software are called *versions*.

A new word-processor might be called WordCrunch 1.0. If it sells well, then the company may issue a revised version, perhaps containing changes to errors in the first version, called WordCrunch 1.1. After a year or so, the whole package might be completely revised, with the addition of new features, such as perhaps a dictionary in which to look up the spelling of words. This new version might be called WordCrunch 2.0. And so on.

Later versions are always compatible with the earlier ones, so that a letter written using WordCrunch 1.0 can still be edited using WordCrunch 2.0.

Figure 8.1

This is to ensure that customers who have bought the earlier version can upgrade their software to the new version, without losing all their work.

Piracy

The cost of one software package might be several hundred pounds. But the cost of producing each box is comparatively small – the disks cost less than a pound each to produce, and the books cost a few pounds. Software is expensive because any commercial program is very long and complicated, and it must be tested exhaustively to make sure it works in all circumstances. It costs a great amount of money to write the actual programs, but once they are written it costs very little to produce copies of them.

The consequence is that illegal copying of software is very common, just as is the illegal copying of cassette tapes. Anyone with a computer can make a copy of a disk, for no more than the cost of the disk itself.

Software companies have endeavoured to stamp out piracy of their material. Though copying of commercial disks seems like a victimless crime, if it becomes widespread it means the end of software, for no-one would bother to produce it if they could not sell a large number of authorized copies. For legal reasons, when you buy software what you actually buy is not the program itself but a licence to use it. That licence is restricted to one machine – if you bought ten separate machines and used the program on all of them, say for teaching purposes, then you would be breaking the terms of the licence just as much as if you copied the program and sold the copies to your friends.

The major software firms are very big indeed. If a program is successful, then it soon pays off its production and development costs, and thereafter a box which costs a few pounds to produce can be sold for a few hundred pounds. In fact, in recent years, the production of software has become much more profitable than the production of hardware.

Shareware

It does not require great resources to produce software, but it does require skill and knowledge. A computer buff can write a program at home, just as well as a composer in the attic can write a sonata. But however good the program is, a single person will have difficulty in advertising and marketing it. A way round this is the writing of *shareware*, by which many amateurs and small firms market their software.

When you buy a shareware program, you pay no more than the cost of the disk. You have the right to try out the program for nothing. If you find the program useful, you can register your ownership officially, and you can pay for a more advanced version of the program, together with documents concerning it.

In particular, there are shareware versions of many of the major commercial programs. For example, WordCrunch might be an important word-processing program. There might be a shareware 'clone' of WordCrunch, called PenFriend. The differences between them would be as follows:

- *WordCrunch*: Costs a few hundred pounds to buy, and you get several books of instructions along with it, and the right to ring up the manufacturers if you have difficulties.
- *PenFriend*: Costs a fraction of WordCrunch. It is shareware, so you can try it out for free before you decide to buy it. But you only get a small leaflet of instructions, and not much in the way of telephone support. Neither does it contain the advanced features of WordCrunch.

PenFriend and WordCrunch are compatible with each other. Suppose the computer at work uses WordCrunch for word-processing, but all you can afford for your home computer is PenFriend. You can write a document using WordCrunch at the office, then take it home and work on it with PenFriend. Next day you can take it back to the office and continue work.

Even cheaper than shareware is software which is in the *public domain*. This costs nothing at all – the writer has renounced copyright, and allows people to copy it for nothing. Often though, public domain software consists of technical programs only of interest to computer buffs.

If a computer is joined to a network, then it can receive software directly from other components in the network.

OPERATING SYSTEMS

You start up a computer by switching it on. There is a jargon word for this – it is described as 'booting' the computer. Now, this does not mean that you need to give the computer a good kicking to get it going, but something more metaphysical. The business of starting a computer is, in a way, paradoxical.

Suppose you want to run a word-processing program. The computer needs instructions to load that program, and how to shut it down when you are finished with it, and so on. So as well as the word-processing program, there must be another more fundamental program, telling the computer how to operate the word-processing program.

But somehow this operating program must get started. Beneath the program that operates the word-processing program, there must be a program that operates the operating program. And so on.

We seem to be caught in an infinite regress, of programs to operate programs to operate programs, *ad infinitum*. A computer has to have a process whereby the act of switching on triggers off the operating instructions. This process is described as the computer 'pulling itself up by its bootstraps'. This is where the word 'booting' comes from – computer jargon does sometimes have a certain robust poetry.

In many computers this is called BIOS (Basic Input and Output System). As an ordinary computer user, you do not have to know anything about it, indeed there is no way you can alter it. Once the BIOS is working, programs can be loaded. The first program to be loaded is the one which handles the other programs, and it is called an *operating system*.

Figure 8.2 shows the various programs on top of each other. At the bottom is the BIOS which gets the computer going. Above it is the operating system which runs the applications programs. In this case, a word-processing program is being run. With the word-processor you are writing a document called 'George3', which is perhaps your third letter to George.

The operating system does not itself do any of the useful tasks that you want a computer for, such as word-processing or games-playing. Instead, it does all the 'housekeeping' of the computer, which enables the applications programs to be run efficiently. The tasks include the following:

● Copying data from one disk onto another.

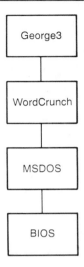

Figure 8.2

- Telling you what files are on a disk.
- Erasing a file from a disk.

There are many operating systems available. Some names are UNIX, PCDOS, CP/M and OS2. UNIX is very commonly used, on processors of all sizes.

In this chapter, we deal mainly with microprocessors, in particular with PCs. The most widely used operating system for PCs is MSDOS (Microsoft Disc Operating System). The instructions in MSDOS for the above tasks are:

- *diskcopy A: B:*   This will copy the contents of the disk in drive A to the disk in drive B.
- *dir B:*   This will print on the screen the names of all the files in the disk in drive B.
- *del troll.exe*   This will erase from the disk the file labelled 'troll.exe'.

FILES

The word *file* covers all the items of software you might find on a disk. There are various sorts of file. Some examples include:

- *Text files*: These contain the actual words, perhaps a letter or an essay, that have been written using a word-processor.
- *Picture files*: These contain, in coded form, pictures that have been created by a graphics program.
- *Program files*: These contain the actual programs that can be run.

Often you can tell the type of a file by looking at the three letters which come after the dot. These three letters are called the *extension*:

- A file labelled 'story.txt' will be a text file.
- A file called 'elf.pcx' will be a picture file, more often than not a picture of an elf. (There are many different ways of coding pictures. The pcx extension indicates that the picture is coded is one particular way.)
- A file labelled 'troll.exe' will be a program file. The extension 'exe' is short for 'execute'. The program itself can be run by typing in 'troll'.

Let us illustrate these by an example. Suppose that you have borrowed a disk from a friend, which contains a game called 'Troll-Slayer'. Let us suppose that this game is shareware, so that you are not breaking the law by copying the game and trying out the game before buying it permanently. Let us further suppose that your computer has two disk-drives.

You will first want to copy the disk, so that you can return the original to your friend. Put the original in drive A and a blank disk of your own in drive B. Type in:

> diskcopy A: B: (don't forget to press 'enter' after the B)

The computer will now copy all the files on the disk in drive A to the disk in drive B. The original disk in drive A can be removed and returned. You now have your own copy of the game.

Perhaps you have forgotten to ask your friend how to start the game. You will need to know what files are on the disk. So type in:

> dir B: (again, don't forget to press 'enter')

You will see a listing of the files on the disk. Among them might be:

- *story.txt*   You can read this to find the background story of the game.
- *elf.pcx*   This will be a picture of an elf which is on the screen for some stage of the game.
- *troll.exe*   This is the actual program which runs the game.

So type in 'troll' and you can get down to the business of slaying trolls.

DIRECTORIES

In the long run, it is very sensible to organize your documents so that they can be found easily. After all, a successful business does not keep all the letters it receives higgledy-piggledy in a box. They are classified and organized so that they can be referred to easily.

Suppose that you have a computer with a hard disk, and that you have been using it to write all your essays and letters, as well as to store a few games and other programs. You may have several hundred files. If you want to refer to a letter you wrote a year ago, it will be very hard to find it among all the others. Unless you have been very systematic, you will not have given the letter a title so that it can be found quickly. Was it 'Letter33'? Or '1991Nov'? Or 'George3'? You may find you are having to look at dozens of documents before you find the one you want.

The way to organize documents on a disk is by putting them in separate *directories*. Each directory may contain several files. It may also contain other directories, called sub-directories. For example, you may have a directory labelled 'Letters'. This may contain all your letters, if you don't write very many. But it may contain several sub-directories, one containing letters to friends, another letters connected with business, and so on. Perhaps the business-letter sub-directory may contain sub-sub-directories, and so on.

So we see that directories are linked in a hierarchy. The directory at the origin of the hierarchy is the *root* directory, and it is the one you are in when the computer is booted. It will contain the basic instructions of the operating system, and the names of the directories which are in the next level of the hierarchy.

Let us take the directory hierarchy (called directory *tree*) of someone who is using a computer to help in the production of a magazine of which he is editor. He might want to organize the material in the following way:

- *Articles* which appeared in the magazine, divided by the year in which they appeared.
- *Correspondence* concerning the magazine, again divided by year.
- *Financial documents* concerning the magazine.

The tree structure corresponding to this is shown below.

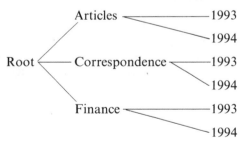

You can introduce new directories. To continue the example above, at the beginning of 1995, we will want to introduce new directories to keep the 1995 articles separate from the previous year's. How this is done will depend on the system being used.

GUI

GUI stands for Graphical User Interface. You are the user, and the interface between you and the computer is in the form of a picture as opposed to letters.

In an operating system such as MSDOS, instructions are entered by the keyboard. Another way of giving instructions to the computer is by a *mouse*. This is a small item of hardware described in the previous chapter – it is held in the hand and moved across a table, which causes a pointer to move across the screen. When the pointer has reached the place you want, you press one of the buttons on top of the mouse to perform a task. This is easier than having to type in the instructions for the task.

The operating systems described so far, MSDOS and so on, are generally thought not to be user-friendly. When you want to do something you have to type in the instructions, and the words used may be unnatural and abbreviated. To continue the example above, suppose that an article, called XYZ, has been misfiled, in one of the correspondence directories instead of the article directories. In order to move it we have to copy it from the old directory to the new, and then delete it in the old directory. The MSDOS commands are:

$$\text{copy} \setminus \text{corres} \setminus 1993 \setminus \text{XYZ article} \setminus 1993 \setminus$$
$$\text{del} \setminus \text{corres} \setminus 1993 \setminus \text{XYZ}$$

Though computers can work very quickly and accurately, they are not intelligent in their own right. They recognize only precise instructions. If you type the instructions above incorrectly, it will refuse to act upon them.

The rules are given in the user's manual, but the examples given are often not very helpful. Someone who is not a computer expert will have to look up the correct instruction, and often try many versions before it is typed in exactly the correct form. To do more than the basic operations requires considerable knowledge and expertise.

With a more visual and intuitive system there is less chance of going wrong, and beginners can use the system with more confidence. The components which describe a GUI system are described by the word WIMP.

WIMP

This stands for Window Icon Menu Pointer. Let us take each of these in turn:

- A *window* is an area of the screen on which you are working. It can occupy the whole screen or just a part of it. You can have more than one window on the screen at the same time if you are dealing with more than one task at a time, and you can switch between these tasks.
- The *icon* is a little symbol on the screen, about $\frac{1}{2}''$ square. It might be a picture of an artist's palette, or a sheet of text, or a solitaire board. The palette indicates a drawing program, the text a word-processing program, the solitaire board a game program.

- Often you have several choices. You might want to start a new letter, or to change one you have already written. A list of these choices will appear on the screen, and this list is called the *menu*.
- The mouse controls a *pointer*, perhaps shaped like an arrow, which can be moved about the screen. You can use it to select which window you want to work on, or which icon to pick, or which item from a menu to choose. Just point the pointer at the thing you want and press one of the buttons of the mouse.

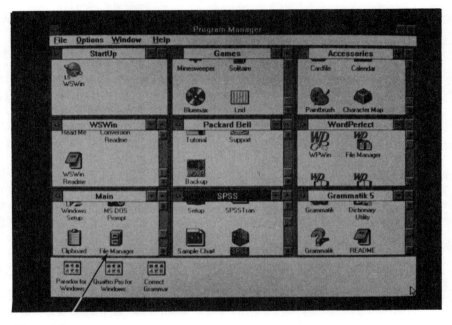

Figure 8.3

Let us see how the use of WIMP simplifies the example above of moving a file from one place to another. When you start up a Windows session, you may see a Program Manager screen like the one shown in Fig. 8.3.

There is an icon like a filing cabinet, labelled 'file manager'. This enables you to control your files. Point at this icon, and press one of the mouse buttons. You may then see a list of files and directories. Position the pointer over the file you want to move, and press the mouse button. While the button is still depressed, move the pointer until it is over the correct directory (this is called *dragging* the file) and release the button. The file will now be moved to where you want it.

This method may not be quicker than typing in commands, but it is more fool-proof.

Running more than one program

Big computers can be used by many people at the same time. A university computer will be used simultaneously by the administration and by the various departments. There is a complicated system of time-sharing so that the computer can switch between different tasks, and each user can imagine that the computer is working for him or her alone. This operation is *multitasking*. Big mainframe computers can perform this operation, but smaller microcomputers, by and large, can only do one thing at a time.

This is inconvenient for many commercial users. While writing a report using a word-processing program, you might want to do some calculations connected with the report. You might want to construct a chart, to be inserted in the report. You might want to refer to the list of data on which the report is based. It takes a long time to leave the word-processing program, start up the spreadsheet to make the chart, then return to the word-processor. It would be convenient to have all these tasks active simultaneously.

Windows is a system that enables you to have several jobs going at the same time. It is graphical, so you don't have to remember complicated DOS instructions. It is itself an operating system, one that sits on top of the DOS.

The system stems from one invented by Xerox in 1981. It became used widely on Macintosh microcomputers, and then on IBM-compatible computers when Microsoft developed their version. It requires a fast computer with a great deal of memory – after all, if you are doing several tasks, the computer needs to keep all their details in its memory. Running a task under Windows is slower and requires more memory than running under the ordinary operating system, but nowadays hardware is cheap and people are expensive (quite the opposite from a few years ago) and the use of Windows enables many more people to use computers efficiently.

Another advantage is that of standardization. When applications are run in a Windows environment, the rules for various tasks such as opening and closing them are standardized. So the user does not have to remember or look up the instructions for each one.

BUGS AND VIRUSES

Bugs

A commercial program is a very complicated thing, containing thousands of instructions. When it is first written, it will almost certainly contain mistakes. These might be simple typing errors, or they might be logical errors which make the computer do the wrong thing altogether. The program will be tested again and again, but it is always likely that mistakes remain. These mistakes are called *bugs*.

A new commercial program may contain several bugs, and these will be discovered by the people who bought it. They will inform the software firm, who will rewrite the program so that the bugs are eliminated. A new version of the program (see pp. 115–16) will contain the corrections. Often though it takes a while before all the bugs are discovered.

Viruses

No computer programmer includes bugs on purpose. They just arise from the errors human beings make when carrying out an enormously complicated project. Viruses, by contrast, are written deliberately. They are written to hamper or even destroy the work of other computer users.

One virus, known as 'Stoned' or 'New Zealand', is activated every tenth time the computer is switched on. The message 'This PC is stoned' appears on the screen, and you have to switch off and start again. Another virus is such that the user has to type in 'Happy Birthday Joshi' before the computer will work.

These viruses are obviously very irritating, but they do not seriously damage the work you want to do. The motives of the writers of these viruses are obvious – Joshi, for example, must be very pleased at the thought of being wished Happy Birthday by thousands of people across the globe.

Other viruses are more serious. They can act to slow down the computer so that it is almost useless, or they can erase the data written on disks. It is difficult to imagine what motivates the highly intelligent but malevolent writers of such viruses.

So a virus is itself a program. Once it is loaded on a disk (i.e. the disk has become infected), it attaches itself to another program. So whenever the other program is run the virus is activated. This is not all. The virus program contains instructions to reproduce itself, and copy itself onto any other disk put into the computer. So if the hard disk of your machine is infected, it may contaminate any floppy disk that you use.

Infection

How do you catch viruses? They are transmitted on disks or through other electronic media. If you buy a software disk from an established company, it will have been rigorously checked for viruses and you can be confident that it is clean. But if you borrow a disk from someone else, or buy pirated software, then the disk may be infected. One virus was carried on a disk which contained information about AIDS – there is an uncomfortably close analogy between computer viruses and sexually transmitted diseases.

Viruses can also be transmitted over networks and over the telephone system. One virus spread from coast to coast of the USA in a few hours.

Inoculation

How do you prevent your computer catching viruses? One way, of course, is to make sure that you only use software that has come from safe sources. But if you like to obtain software from your friends, then your computer is liable to infection. There are programs on the market (which continue the disease analogy by acting rather like inoculation) which recognize all the common viruses. If you have one of these programs installed on your machine, then it will check every disk put into the drive, and report on whether it has found the code corresponding to a virus. If it does, it will prevent the virus program being transmitted to the computer.

Cure

If your computer has caught a virus, what can you do about it? Is there a cure? That depends on the sophistication of the virus. If it is one of the comparatively simple ones, then one of the anti-virus programs may be able to eradicate it from your hard disc. If it is a new virus, or a more complicated one, then disinfection may be impossible. What is also possible is that by the time you realize you have caught a virus, it has done its destructive work of erasing a vast amount of the work you have done. However clever an anti-virus program is, it cannot restore information that has been rubbed off.

Although scare stories in the press have exaggerated the danger of viruses, you must decide for yourself how thoroughly you need to protect your system against them. They are not that common, and most of them are irritating rather than destructive. But it is worth taking precautions against them, just in case you are caught off guard and lose several months' work. A simple practice that reduces the peril of viruses and mechanical breakdown alike is that of *backing up*.

All this involves is making back-up copies of your work. Whenever you have done a substantial amount of work, make a copy of it on a floppy disk or another storage device. Then if you do catch a virus, or if your hard disk breaks down, all you have lost will be what you have written since you last backed-up.

INSTALLATION

Suppose you have bought a software package. It will come with instructions on how to get it up and running, but these are not always easy for the beginner to follow. Many hours of frustration can follow before your new program is working properly. Below are some of the steps required, if you are using the operating system MSDOS on a PC.

If your computer runs on a floppy disk-drive, or if you want to make a copy of the software disks just in case you make a mistake, you will need to *format* a disk to hold the information. The blank disks that you can buy from shops work for different sorts of computers, and you will have to arrange the recording surface of the disk you buy so that it can hold the information for your particular computer. This operation is known as *formatting*.

Put the blank disk in the disk drive A. The MSDOS command is:

format A: (then press 'enter')

Be careful with this command. If the wrong disk is in the drive, then all the information on that disk will be erased.

The formatting will take a minute or so. You are then ready to install the software. If you are using a hard disk, the instructions will often ask you to make a special directory in which the software will be held. The instruction for this might be:

md wordcrun   (press 'enter')

(md stands for Make Directory)

You then put the software disk in drive A. The instruction to start installing might be:

install a:

You then follow the instructions on the screen. It might ask you to type in the serial number of the package (this is a move to discourage piracy). This number might be on the box in which the software came, or on the first disk provided.

At the end of it all you will want to try out the new software, i.e. to run the program. First you must move to the directory in which you have installed the software. The MSDOS instruction is:

cd \wordcrun   (press 'enter')

(cd stands for Change Directory).

During the installation, you should have been told what instruction word to use. Type it in, and things should run successfully.

The example of software we have given is of a word-processor. How these are used is the subject of the next chapter.

9   Word-processing

Apart from playing games, the reason why most people buy a computer is to do word-processing. It is one of the most common uses, and if you have bought a computer it is likely that you will want to use it for word-processing. One way of describing this function of a computer is to say that it is a very sophisticated form of electronic typewriter, but this is to underestimate its true significance. Because it is so flexible in the way that it can handle text, a word-processing program can benefit considerably the way in which you write. In this chapter, we will describe the *technique* of using a word-processing package, and show how it can help you with the process of writing.

We are using the phrase 'word-processor' to refer not to the machine but to the program that can be run on it. There is a wide range of word-processing packages available, from fairly basic ones which are relatively cheap, to elaborate, expensive ones which come with a great number of extra facilities. In all word-processing programs, though, the basic procedures are the same. First, we shall describe the keyboard which you use to enter your text.

KEYBOARD

The keyboard of a computer contains all the keys that are on an ordinary typewriter. It will also contain many other keys. Figure 9.1 shows a standard PC keyboard. One can see all the keys for the letters and numbers. You will find yourself using many of the other keys.

1. *Shift*, *Ctrl*, *Alt*. The shift key plays the same role as it does on a typewriter. When you hold it down and press a letter, you will get a capital letter. The characters above the number keys are obtained in this way: the % sign is obtained by holding down Shift and pressing the 5 key. The way we describe this key combination is:

    Shift + 5

    The Ctrl (Control) and Alt (Alternative) keys behave similarly. By holding them down and pressing other keys, you can get other symbols,

Figure 9.1

or do different tasks. There are no standard rules for this though. The manual of whatever program you are using will explain what means what. You might find that to make characters italic, you hold down Ctrl and press I. In symbols:

Ctrl + I

2. *Arrow keys.* These keys enable you to move around the screen. They are used in games as well as in serious programs.
3. *Page up, Page down, Home, End.* These keys also move you around the screen. The Home key, for example, may move you to the beginning of the line you are working on. These keys may be used in conjunction with the Shift, Ctrl or Alt keys. Holding down Ctrl and pressing End may move you to the end of whatever you are working on.
4. *Function keys.* Along the top of the keyboard you will see a row of keys labelled F1, F2 up to F12. These perform special functions. Often the F1 key is the 'Help' key: press it and information will appear on the screen to help you with whatever you are doing. There is no standard rules for what function key does what – you have to find that out from the manual.
5. *Number pad.* The group of keys on the right can be used for numbers. In banks, the cashier often uses these keys to enter numbers rather than the keys above the letters.
6. *Other keys.* There are many other keys (there are 102 in total!). Some you will probably never need to use, and others we will explain as we go along.

GUI

Many word-processors can be run under a GUI system such as Windows. They often say as much in their title, for example a version of WordCrunch might be called 'WordCrunch for Windows'. You can move around the document and perform various word-processing tasks with the mouse. For example, you many be able to move to a page further on in the document by placing the pointer over a certain area and clicking.

For the next two sections of this chapter, we shall assume that you have started the program running and are ready to begin typing, a letter or an essay or a novel or whatever.

BASIC WORD-PROCESSING

We will suppose you have switched on and are ready to start work on a word-processor. Most of the screen in front of you is blank. There may be instructions and symbols along the borders, but the central area is like a blank sheet of paper on which you can write. The screen for one word-processing program is shown in Fig. 9.2.

There will be a small symbol flashing on and off in the top-left hand corner of the blank area. This symbol is called the *cursor*, and it indicates where the letters you type in will appear.

So you start typing. The words appear on the screen, just as the words appear on a sheet of paper when you are using an ordinary typewriter. But when you reach the end of a line, you will see how a word-processor is different from (and superior to) a typewriter.

Word-wrap

On an ordinary typewriter, at the end of each line you have to return the carriage to start the next line. Often there is a bell to remind you to do this. A word-processor does this automatically for you. When you have typed enough to fill one line, the cursor automatically starts a new line.This process is called *word-wrap*.

There is still a key which has the effect of returning the carriage. It is used when you want to end a paragraph. For the paragraph above, the only time 'carriage return' was pressed was after the phrase *word-wrap*. All the other lines were ended automatically, without any intervention from the author.

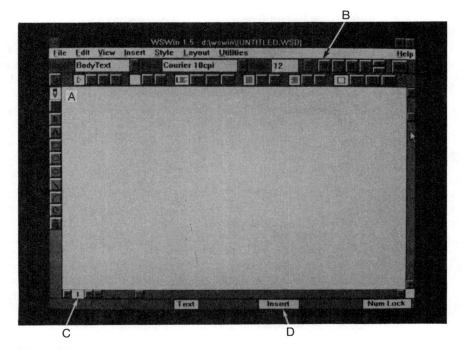

Figure 9.2

Mistakes

Let us suppose that you have typed several lines. Unless you are a monster of accuracy, you will have made a few mistakes in your typing. If you were working on a typewriter, you would have to paint over the mistakes with a correction fluid, wait until it dried, and then type over them. If there were many mistakes, or you had missed out half a dozen words, you would have to scrap what you had done and start all over again.

It is in the correction of mistakes that word-processing first shows its great superiority over ordinary typing. You can correct mistakes quickly, and the final result will look as good as if you had never made the mistake in the first place. On the keyboard you will see a group of four arrows, for up, down, left and right. You can use these arrows to move the cursor to where you made a mistake.

There are usually two keys for removing incorrect letters. The *backspace* key (often marked with an arrow '←') will remove the letter to the left of the cursor. The *delete* key (it may be marked with 'del') will remove the character under the cursor or to the right of it. If there is more than one letter to be removed, then you can do so by holding down the key, but be sure not to hold it down for too long! Once the incorrect letters have been removed, you can type in the correct ones.

Insert and Overstrike

Suppose you are correcting your writing. There are two ways that correct letters can be typed in. If the computer is in *insert* mode, then anything you type in will be inserted in the text, without removing any of the old text. If the computer is in *overstrike* mode, then the new letters will erase the old ones. Usually, you will want to be in insert mode – after all, you can always erase the old letters by using either of the delete keys – but there are occasions when it is more convenient to be in overstrike mode. You can switch between the two modes, usually by pressing a key labelled 'insert'. The border of the screen will contain information to tell you which mode you are in. In Fig. 9.2, notice that the word 'Insert' appears at the bottom of the screen.

Moving around

You can get to any point in your document by using the arrow keys mentioned above. If your document is very long, this will be a tedious procedure. Every word-processing program will contain ways to move quickly around the document. The instructions vary from program to program, but they will include ways to go directly to the following:

- end of line
- beginning of line
- end of page
- beginning of page
- end of document.
- beginning of document.

It is not essential to use these shortcuts. You can get from beginning to end of a document by repeatedly pressing the down arrow. But if your document is a long one, it will take a long time: using the 'end of document' instruction on a fast computer may take less than a second.

Cut/Copy and Paste

Suppose, after writing a piece of work, you want to remove a whole paragraph. Or suppose that you want to move a few lines of explanation to earlier on in the document. If you have done the work on an ordinary typewriter, then often there is no choice but to type the whole thing again. On a word-processor, though, you can either remove or insert great chunks of text, and in the final print out there will be no indication that the document was ever altered.

The procedure depends on the word-processor you are using. But in all cases you have to select the text you are going to remove or move. In some cases, this is done by setting markers at the beginning and end of the text.

You will then see the selected text highlighted or appear in a different colour. There are then different routines for the following:

1. Copying the selected text.
2. Moving the selected text.
3. Deleting the selected text.

For (2) and (3) the selected text will disappear. If you want to delete the text, then the operation is over and you can continue with some other task. If you want to move the text or copy it, then put the cursor at the place where you want the new position to start, and there will be a routine to insert the text in its new place.

Italics **Bold** <u>Underline</u>

You can add emphasis to your writing by putting words in *italics*, or in **bold** type, or by <u>underlining</u> them. Again, the procedure varies from one word-processor to another. In some cases, you put markers at the beginning and end of the word you want to be in italics. This might be done by pressing $+I$ at the beginning and $-I$ at the end.

In other cases, there are different procedures for whether you want to italicize new words, or italicize a section of text that you have already written. If you want to start writing in bold, then press the appropriate key or keys (which might be Ctrl + B in one system, or f6 in another), type in the text, then press the appropriate key again once you want the bold section to end. If you want to embolden something already written, then select the words by the procedure described above, and then press the appropriate key or keys to make it bold.

Find and Replace/Find and Exchange

Often you want to change the same word many times in a document. You might have written something about a person called Davies, and then realize that you should have spelled his name as Davis. To go through the document changing each example might be very tedious, and it would be easy to miss one case. The facility of 'Find and Replace' or 'Find and Exchange' will enable you to change all the occurrences in one go.

Again, the precise routine will vary from system to system. But you are asked to say what word you want found, and what you want to replace it by. Usually, you are given the choice of confirming each exchange (after all, there might be someone else in your document whose name really is spelt Davies) or of doing the whole thing automatically.

The example just given applied to correcting a mistake. But the Find and Replace facility has other uses. Suppose you are writing a story in which you haven't yet decided on the name of the main character. You can call your character '**'. Then when you have decided on her name, Dolores say, you can use the Find and Replace facility automatically to replace '**' by 'Dolores' thoughout the whole story.

Line spacing

For many purposes you will often want to have lines widely spaced. For example, it makes it easier to correct a document if there is space between the lines. There will be a routine for having, say, double spacing, in which there is twice the usual gap between lines. In some circumstances, for example if you want to type fractional expressions, you will want to have less than the usual spacing. There may be a facility for doing this.

Letter size and spacing

You may be able to alter the size of the letters. This is measured in *points*, where there are 72 points per inch. So if the size of your letters is 12 point, then you will get 6 letters per inch.

When you use a typewriter, each letter is allotted the same amount of space. This makes the i's look isolated, and the m's and w's cramped. On a word processor, you can select *proportional spacing*, so that different letters are given different amounts of space.

On a typewriter, the lengths of the lines vary. On a word-processor, you can make the text *justified*, which means that each line has the same length. The difference between lines is accommodated by adjusting the gaps between words.

With justification and proportional spacing, your work looks much more like printed text, so that the final result does not differ greatly from the pages of a book.

Templates

Often you will be writing the same sort of document many times. For example, every time you write a personal letter you will want to have your address at the top. It is a nuisance to have to type this in for every letter, and you can create a standard letter form which can be used over and over again. This standard form is called a *template*. Whenever you start a letter based on this template, your address will appear at the top of the page without you having to type it in.

The template we have just described is for writing your personal letters. They can be less detailed. They might just ensure that the document you write is in the form you want, with the correct line spacing, justification, and so on.

Templates are also used in other applications, for example in graphics programs. You might be creating many diagrams which have lots of features in common. You could prepare a *template* picture which contained all these common features and nothing more. When you do one of the individual pictures you only have to insert those features which make it different from the template.

GUI

As mentioned earlier, many of the tasks described above can be carried out by pointing, clicking and *dragging* the mouse. For example, if you want to make some text **bold**, you can do this by clicking on the bold symbol on the border of the screen and then typing in the text. In Fig. 9.2, there is a little square with a B on it.

If you wish to copy or delete a section of text, you can do this by positioning the pointer at the beginning of the section, holding down one of the buttons, and moving the mouse so that the pointer moves to the end of the passage. This is known as *dragging*. You will then find that the passage is highlighted, and the alterations that you want will be applied to that passage.

In the bottom left-hand corner of Fig. 9.2, there is the page number with two little arrows on either side of it. Clicking on the right of these arrows will move through the document by one page.

ADVANCED FACILITIES

The features described so far are common to virtually all word-processors. Some of the following features may not be on the cheaper sort of word-processor.

Spell-check

A spell-check looks through your document and picks out any word that it thinks is misspelled. This requires sufficient memory on the computer to contain a dictionary, because the spell-check is examining each word that you have written and seeing whether it is in its dictionary. If it can't find a word, then it will offer you alternatives. Sometimes the alternatives are based on an *alphabetical* principle, of being correct words which are close in an alphabetic order to what you have typed. Sometimes they are *phonetic*, based on words which sound like what you have typed. Often the correct word is not shown, in which case you can type in what you want.

Two things can go wrong with a spell-check. It can fail to pick out mistakes, and it can pick out as an error what is perfectly correct. Since computers cannot read text as intelligently as humans, there is no way to avoid the first drawback. It is very easy to write 'form' when you mean 'from', and as both of these are correct words the spell-check will not notice the mistake. On the other hand, if you are writing about someone with an unusual name, then the spell-check will stop at each occurrence and offer a suggestion, often amusing, of how that person's name should be spelt. But you will be able to add that name to the dictionary, so that the spell-check will regard it as a correctly spelt word.

Thesaurus

A thesaurus offers you synonyms of a word, i.e. other words which have approximately the same meaning. Say you are writing a horror story, and are sick of using the word 'atrocious' over and over again. The thesaurus will offer you a selection of words which mean roughly the same, all the way from *barbaric* and *brutal* to *vicious* and *wicked*.

Grammar-check

This is similar to a spell-check. It checks your prose for grammatical or stylistic mistakes. Opinions of the value of this facility differ.

Any grammar-check, however sophisticated, cannot have any notion of good style, although it should have a notion of correct grammar. Below are two passages. One of them could have come from an undergraduate essay. The other is one of the most striking passages of English prose, from Edmund Burke's *Reflections on the Revolution in France* (1790).

> The teacher's role in the teaching of reading not only involves providing a variety of experiences but to provide a balanced programme of instruction. The teacher's role is therefore to be a guide to the child and aim to ensure pleasure, understanding, appreciation of organisation and recognising letters are successfully accomplished.

> I thought ten thousand swords must have leaped from their scabbards to avenge even a look that threatened her with insult. – But the age of chivalry is gone. – That of sophisters, economists, and calculators, has succeeded; and the glory of Europe is extinguished for ever. Never, never more, shall we behold that generous loyalty to rank and sex, that proud submission, that dignified obedience, that subordination of the heart, which kept alive, even in servitude itself, the spirit of an exalted freedom. The unbought grace of life, the cheap defence of

nations, the nurse of manly sentiment and heroic enterprise is gone! It is gone, that sensibility of principle, that chastity of honour, which felt a stain like a wound, which inspired courage whilst it mitigated ferocity, which ennobled whatever it touched, and under which vice itself lost half its evil, by losing all its grossness.

We tried a grammar-check on both passages. The first passage was given a clean bill of health even though the authors consider it to contain serious grammatical errors. The grammar-checker was, however, much less approving of the second passage. It said that the full stop after 'insult' should be removed. 'Alive' should be changed to an adverb. All the sentences were rebuked for being too long. The program finally suggested that E. Burke should consider whether he meant 'principle' or 'principal'.

Fonts

The *font* of a letter refers to its actual shape. The word comes from the days when printing was done by making the letters out of metal, so that the letters had to be *founded*, i.e. cast. There are many hundreds of different fonts, some of which may be available on your word-processor. Some are:

Courier

Univers

Times New Roman

Even if your word-processor has different fonts available, your printer may not be able to show them (see pp. 141–2).

WYSIWYG

This stands for 'What You See Is What You Get'. The screen shows more or less what will be printed out on paper. This is very useful when planning a document.

You will not always want your document to be in WYSIWYG mode. In this mode, you cannot see the various codes which put text in italics, or underline words. But you can switch between the WYSIWYG mode and a mode in which all these codes are shown, so that you can delete them if necessary.

Graphics, charts, tables

On the more advanced word-processing programs you can insert pictures, graphs, or tables of numbers. Often you can create these by another application (a graphics program to create the picture, or a spreadsheet to create the table) and insert them into your document. This is often a very complicated procedure and we will not attempt to describe it here.

Desk-Top Publishing

This is an appropriate place to mention Desk-Top Publishing (DTP). This is a name given to a program which enables you to set out the page exactly as you want it, with different columns, paragraphs in boxes separate from the main text, pictures inserted, headlines in large type. A DTP program is a sort of super-word-processor, and there is no absolute boundary between it and ordinary word-processors. Many of the more elaborate word-processors have several of the features of DTP programs, such as being able to insert pictures, or have separate columns of text.

We have mentioned only some of the advanced features that may appear on a word-processor. There are many others, for example facilities to build up an index or table of contents, or to insert footnotes and references to a bibliography.

FILE HANDLING

In the previous two sections, we have discussed what you can do while actually typing. But before you do this you need to start the word-processing program, and when you are satisfied with what you have written you need to finish your session at the computer. Often you will need to reorganize everything you have written into a convenient arrangement, so that you can find what you want quickly.

Starting

Sometimes your word-processing program will be started just by switching on the computer. If you use your computer for other tasks, though, you may have to specify that it is word-processing that you want to do and not any other job. You must use the operating system, as described in the previous chapter, to load the program you want. In the previous chapter, we also discussed the making and ordering of directories. Perhaps your program is called WordCrunch, and you have kept it in a directory called wordcrun. The command to start the program might be 'wc', i.e. there is a file called 'wc.exe' in the directory. The steps to get going might be:

       cd\wordcrun   (to move to the directory containing the program)
             wc   (to start the program).

If you are working within Windows, you can start word-processing by clicking on the icon, which represents the program. Figure 8.3 shows a picture of a Program Manager screen. To start 'Wordperfect', for example, you click on the icon on the right of the screen.

However you have started up the word-processor, you have now two possibilities – you can *open* or *edit* a document that you have been working on previously, or you can *start* or *create* a new document. If you want to open an old document, you have to type in its name or find it from a list of documents presented in front of you. If you want to start a new document, then either you give it a name and then start work on it, or if there is a blank sheet in front of you just start typing.

You now proceed as described in the previous two sections.

Ending

You have finished work for the day. Either you have finished the document you are working on, or you must stop working on it and continue later. You will want to end the word-processing program and switch off the computer.

There will be a command called 'Quit' or 'End' which does this. But you must be careful. Recall that any work you have done will be kept on the RAM of the computer, and that it will be lost the moment you switch off the computer. Before doing this, therefore, you must save the work on some permanent method of storage.

Usually, you will be reminded to save your work before leaving the word-processing program. You can save it on a floppy disk, or on a hard disk if you have one. If you have been editing a previous document, then it will be saved under its previous name; if you have just started a new document, then you may have to give it a name before saving. It is often a good idea to save on both hard and floppy disk (or on two floppy disks). After all, a document might contain 20 hours' work, and that will be lost if the disk becomes faulty.

Organizing documents

After you have been using a computer for a few months, you will have accumulated an impressive amount of work. You may have typed in a 100 letters and essays. Your work will be much more efficient if you organize everything in a systematic way. This means giving your documents names by which they can easily be identified, and arranging them in directories which are sufficiently small for you to find them easily.

Suppose you are an undergraduate whose subjects are politics and philosophy. Suppose that you decide to keep all your academic work on the hard disk of your computer. The main directory for this work is called

Academic. The main divisions or sub-directories that you wish to create under *Academic* are as follows: *notes, lectures, essays, dissertation, bibliography.* Each of these sub-directories will have further sub-directories. For example, you may wish to organize lectures under *subject* and then under *year.* The dissertation sub-directory may well contain sub-directories for *chapters.* The directory tree will now look like this:

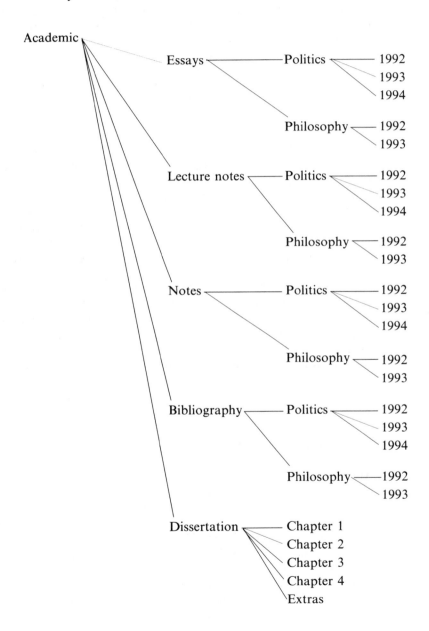

Import and export of documents

Let us say you have written a story, using your WordCrunch program. If the story has been accepted by a magazine, you will want to send a disk containing the story so that it can be printed on the magazine's system. Or you might want it to be worked on by a colleague who has a different word-processing program. Or you might have changed your computer, and have moved up from the basic WordCrunch to the more advanced VerbSap system.

In all these cases, you will want to convert the WordCrunch document to a form which can be read by another word-processing program. This is called *exporting* the document. At the other end, the process of receiving the WordCrunch document is called *importing* it.

It may be that the two word-processing systems are compatible. For example, a document written under the shareware PenFriend program can be read directly under WordCrunch. Or it may be that the importing program can accommodate the documents of other systems. Perhaps VerbSap, being a large complicated program with lots of facilities, can receive documents written in WordCrunch and translate them. In these cases, there is no difficulty in exporting or importing documents.

If the two programs are not compatible, then you can still transfer nearly all of what you have written. There is a highest common factor of word-processing. Virtually all word-processing programs use the same code for the basic alphabet. The code number 65, for example, will always stand for capital A.

This code is called ASCII, which stands for American Standard Code for Information Interchange. It allots numbers to all the letters, spaces, punctuation marks, and so on. It does not include codes to show when a word is in italics, or bold, or of a larger size than the rest. So if you export your document as ASCII, then you will preserve all the actual words you have written. At the other end, if you import a file written in ASCII, you will have all the text preserved, but you will have to reinsert any special effects like italics, Greek letters, and so on.

PRINTING

In most cases, you will want a permanent record of what you have written. You will want to print it out on paper. In the jargon of the trade, you will want a *hard copy*. In Chapter 7, we described the different sorts of printer. The quality of your printer affects not only how your document looks, but also what you can print.

Say you have a fairly elaborate word-processing program. On the screen you may be able to produce many special effects, like different type faces, large letters, Greek or Cyrillic characters. But if your printer is a basic one, it may not be able to print out everything that you have done.

The thing to realize is that when the computer is printing out a document, it is not sending to the printer an exact picture of what is on the screen of the computer. That would be far too slow for most practical purposes. It is sending to the printer the code which describes the characters of the document. The printer receives the code, and provided that it can understand the code, the correct character will be printed out.

If the character is a capital A, then there will be no problem. But if the character is the Greek letter α, say, then the printer may not recognize it. Perhaps it will leave a blank space, or it might print out some other symbol. The printer can only produce the Greek alphabet if it contains the ability to recognize these characters.

Similarly, on the screen you may have written something in a different font. You might want to give a special effect by *making a passage look as if it were handwritten*. (Called *script* font.) When you print this passage, it may come out in the same font as the rest of the document. The printer will only be able to print characters in this special font if it contains sufficient electronic equipment to recognize and produce these characters.

So a simple printer will only be able to print those characters which it already knows. This will be limited to the Roman alphabet, together with a few extra symbols. There will only be a couple of fonts available.

An expensive printer will be able to produce a much wider range of characters. This can be done in two ways. The printer may recognize directly all the other alphabets, symbols and different fonts. Then it can print out an α (Greek alpha) or an ℵ (Hebrew aleph) as easily as it prints out a capital A. In some cases, it is possible to operate a printer in *download* mode. This means that the computer is able to tell the printer exactly what the shape of these extra symbols is. So even if the printer does not have the letter α in its capacity, it can learn from the computer how to print it.

Installing

Before you can print out a document, you must prepare the computer for the particular model of printer you are going to use. This is called *installing* the printer. This is necessary because different printers receive information in different ways, and you must make sure that the computer sends code in the correct format.

The process of installation is usually quite simple. You will be presented with a list of printers, and asked to select the one you have got. There is nothing to stop you installing more than one printer – you might have your own printer for everyday use, but occasionally borrow a more elaborate one for presentation work.

WRITING WITH A WORD-PROCESSOR

Using a word-processor allows you to integrate all the stages of writing onto the screen. You can work in the same document from the moment that you draft preliminary notes and plans until the time when you are ready to submit a completed essay or dissertation. Because it is so easy to delete or to change text on the screen, it is far less effort to try out different versions on the word-processor than it is on a piece of paper. If you wish to make a significant change to a draft, you do not have to write the whole thing out again (including the bits that you *don't* want to change), but you simply delete what you wish to remove and insert the new or additional material. If you want to transfer the position of some passages within an essay, or if you want to move paragraphs from one chapter to another, you do not have to rewrite or use scissors and paste. Instead, you can use the electronic Cut and Paste technique described earlier. This means that in practice you have enough time available to try out several ideas before you settle on the final version. Let us see how this works out in an example.

You have to produce a dissertation as part of your final year assessment in your major subject. There will be a number of stages to go through before you complete your dissertation. First, you will need to plan, in broad outline, what your dissertation is going to look like. Then you will need to review the relevant literature and maybe alter your outline as a result. You may have to access and analyse a database containing data on the subject of your dissertation. Finally, you need to write up the dissertation, incorporating the data analysis, footnotes and bibliography. All this will have to be done regardless of whether you are using a word-processor. But you will be greatly helped if you can use a computer, and can do it all on screen as an integrated process.

We don't want to tell you exactly how you should write a dissertation, but you might begin by drafting a plan which takes the equivalent of a side of A4 paper. This might consist of no more than a few sentences outlining your main ideas and a set of chapter headings. When you have done this, you should save your thoughts on disk. You should then print out a hard copy and put it in your dissertation file.

The next thing you might want to do is to carry out a review of the published material on your topic. You could open a new document and type your notes directly into the computer, making sure to save your writing and to print a hard copy. Perhaps you would then draft the first couple of chapters, based on your review. You can write these secure in the knowledge that they will be easy to alter if and when the need arises. If there are parts that you are not yet ready to write, or you are dubious about, then you can easily signal this by a note in a different font or in italics.

If you have a powerful word-processing package, then you can build up footnotes and references while you draft the dissertation. If you add extra footnotes, then they will be inserted automatically between the previous ones and the notes will be renumbered. A bibliography facility will automatically arrange your references in alphabetical order.

This example shows how powerful a good word-processing package can be. When it is combined with facilities for importing text from other documents, or tables and graphics produced by other packages, it becomes more powerful still. When operating in a Windows environment, it becomes easy to integrate the elements produced by different packages.

Word-processing gives you two great advantages over conventional writing. First, it enables you to write in a more relaxed and exploratory way than with pen and paper. Second, it saves your time: the hours that would otherwise be occupied by routine clerical tasks can be spent in thinking and trying out ideas.

10   Spreadsheets

The sequence of instructions that make a computer do something is a program. The first programmers were highly skilled mathematicians. Though many people can now program a computer, at the basic level at least, the task of writing a useful program is one that requires a great deal of training and practice.

Many more people need to use computers than have the time, inclination or temperament to learn programming. They can do word-processing, and this application can be learnt without knowing anything of the underlying program. People can use a database to handle vast quantities of information, without knowing how it is constructed. A *spreadsheet* is another computer application that enables people to perform very involved calculations without having to program the computer to do so.

Fewer people are aware of spreadsheets than of other applications. Everyone is familiar with a typewriter, and can understand that a word-processor is an extension of this. One can also imagine a database program as an electronic filing-cabinet. But there is no everyday analogy for a spreadsheet. Perhaps the nearest common object is a calculator, and indeed the first spreadsheet program was called Visicalc.

Spreadsheets are becoming more widely used, however. A great amount of mathematical investigation can be done on a spreadsheet, and so they have a place in education as well as in business. One can pick up the basics of spreadsheets very quickly, so that one can be doing useful things after only a few hours of training.

SPREADSHEET BASICS

When you start up a spreadsheet program, you will see that the screen is divided into a grid of rectangles. Each of these rectangles is a *cell*. Each cell has a label, or *address*. How these addresses are given varies, but for the most part the columns have a letter, and the rows a number. The address of a cell can be given by its column letter and row number. The one shaded in Fig. 10.1 is cell C5. On the border of the screen the active cell will be named, as shown.

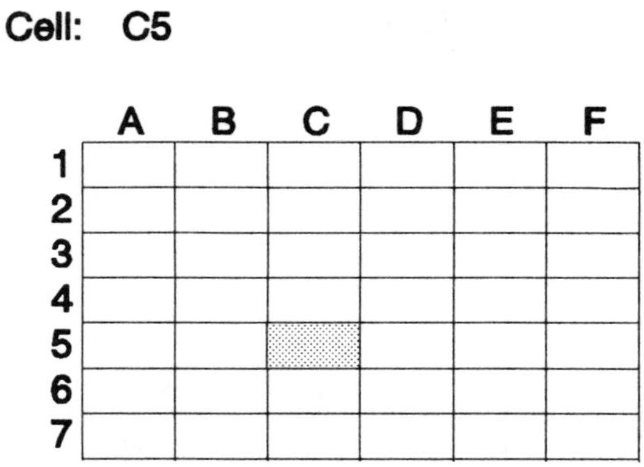

Cell: C5

Figure 10.1

The spreadsheet will be much larger than what you see on the screen. It depends on the program, but you might have 8000 columns and 8000 rows available to you. One can think of the spreadsheet as a gigantic sheet of paper, with a grid drawn on it. Only a small part of the grid is being shown on the screen.

Entry

Just as you can write on paper, you can enter things into the cells of the spreadsheet. At any time there will be one cell which is ready to receive your entries. This is the *active* cell, and is shown by being lit up in some way. On the border of the screen you will see which cell is active: in Fig. 10.1 it is C5.

There are three sorts of thing you could enter: text, numbers and formulas.

Text

In each cell you can enter ordinary words. They might be the names of people, or of books, or of items in a warehouse. It doesn't matter if the name is too long to be displayed in the cell, as you can expand the column to accommodate it.

Let us suppose that we are using the spreadsheet to list the purchases we might make to set up a computer system. Down the first column we will have the names of the items. So in cell A1 type in 'computer'. Use the down-arrow to go to cell A2, and there type in 'printer'. And so on. After all the items have been listed, the spreadsheet will look something like that in Fig. 10.2.

	A	B	C	D	E	F
1	computer					
2	printer					
3	cable					
4	cover					
5	paper					
6						
7						

Figure 10.2

Numbers

In each cell you can enter ordinary numbers. They can be whole numbers or fractional.

To continue our example above, we might want to list the prices of all the items. So in cell B1 type in 680, which is the price in pounds of the computer. Again, use the down-arrow to reach cell B2, and type in 450. After typing in all the prices the spreadsheet will be as shown in Fig. 10.3.

	A	B	C	D	E	F
1	computer	680				
2	printer	450				
3	cable	14				
4	cover	8.45				
5	paper	22.99				
6						
7						

Figure 10.3

Some spreadsheets require you to put an '=' sign before the number (just in case the computer thinks you are referring to a person, a Mr 680 say), but usually the computer will recognize the entry as a number.

Formulas

By entering names and numbers on a spreadsheet, we are not doing anything that could not be done on an ordinary sheet of paper. But a spreadsheet is much more than a great blank space on which to write. It can be regarded as *calculating* paper, which can evaluate the various expressions that may be written on it.

You write the expression much as you do an ordinary mathematical expression. There are a few things to watch out for.

1. Multiplication is shown by the '*' symbol. So 'two times two' is written '2*2'.
2. Suppose you want to apply a formula to the contents of another cell. Suppose your active cell is G9, and you want to add 5 to another cell, say F8. You can then type in 5+F8, and the result displayed in G9 will be 5 greater than whatever number is in F8.
3. If a formula begins with a cell address, as say F8+5, then you must let the computer know you are typing in a formula not a name (just in case there is a Mr F8+5). To do so put a '+' in front of the formula (or '=' in the case of EXCEL).
4. You type in the formula, but what appears in the cell is not the formula itself but its result. Suppose that cell F8 contains the number 12. Then after typing in +F8+5 in the active cell G9, what you see in cell G9 is the result of the formula, 17. If you want to check the formula, it does appear on the border of the screen.

Let us continue our example. The price list in the B column refers to prices before value added tax (VAT) was added. Let us use the C column to enter the VAT. You do not have to do any calculation, the spreadsheet will do it all for you. You want to find the VAT of each price, at a rate of 17.5%. So you multiply each price by $\frac{17.5}{100} = 0.175$. In cell C1, enter the formula which will multiply the entry in cell B1 by this amount. The formula is:

$$+ \text{B1*0.175}$$

The spreadsheet will now look as shown in Fig. 10.4. Notice that the entry in C1 is not the formula, but the result of applying that formula to the entry in B1, $680 \times 0.175 = 119$. If you want to check the formula, it does appear on the border of the screen as shown.

This does not seem much quicker than using a calculator to work out the VAT. It seems that we will have to type in similar formulas for each of the other items. But a spreadsheet contains a method to do all these calculations in one go.

COPYING FORMULAS

Continuing the example above, we will want to calculate the VAT for all the other items on the list. If we continue to do it by the same formula, cell C2 will contain an expression which multiplies the entry in B2 by 0.175, i.e.

Cell: C1   +B1*0.175

	A	B	C	D	E	F
1	computer	680	119			
2	printer	450				
3	cable	14				
4	cover	8.45				
5	paper	22.99				
6						
7						

Figure 10.4

it will contain +B2*0.175. Similarly, C3 will contain +B3*0.175, and so on down the list.

If we had to type in these new formulas individually, then indeed no time would be saved by using a spreadsheet. But every spreadsheet contains a 'copy' facility, to copy the formula in C1 down the rest of the column. The instructions vary depending on what program you are using, but they will require you to do the following:

- Say that you want to 'copy'.
- Give the cell or cells you want to copy from (in this case, C1).
- Give the cell or cells you want to copy to (in this case, C2 to C5).

You will then see the formula copied down the column, as shown in Fig. 10.5. Make the active cell C2, the one below C1. Note that a very clever thing has happened. The formula has been copied with the slight changes that you wanted it to have. The formula in cell C2 is not an exact copy of the one in C1. It has been amended, to take account of the fact that you have moved down a row, by changing the B1 in the formula to B2, and so on. If you look at the formulas in the rest of the C column, you will see that they have all been changed so that they refer to the cell on their left.

In the examples so far, we have copied only a single cell. We can copy a whole row of cells, or a column, or even a whole block. Figure 10.6 shows a row, a column and a block. You refer to them as follows:

- Row: cells C2..E2
- Column: cells A3..A5
- Block: cells C4..E7

The only restriction, in fact, is that you cannot copy an irregular shape. You have to split it up into rectangles and copy them individually.

Cell: C2   +B2*0.175

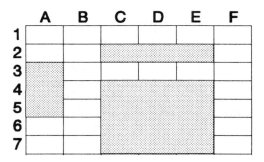

	A	B	C	D	E	F
1	computer	680	119			
2	printer	450	78.75			
3	cable	14	2.45			
4	cover	8.45	1.48			
5	paper	22.99	4.02			
6						
7						

Figure 10.5

	A	B	C	D	E	F
1						
2						
3						
4						
5						
6						
7						

Figure 10.6

Addresses

The position of a cell is its address, given by the column and the row that it belongs to. There are two ways of stating addresses. An *absolute* address gives a definite cell on the grid; a *relative* address gives the position of a cell in relation to another cell. Usually, we want relative addresses. The computer will assume that any address is relative unless you tell it otherwise.

Relative addresses

This notion of *relative* and *absolute* addressing is central to the use of spreadsheets. To emphasize the example above, in cell C1 we entered the formula +B1*0.175. The address B1 in this formula refers to the cell, not with absolute address B1, but with address B1 *relative* to C1. In this case, the relative address B1 means: 'The cell one to the left'.

So this explains why the formula changed when it was copied down the column. When it was copied to cell C2, the relative address 'The cell one to the left' referred to B2. So the formula changed to +B2*0.175.

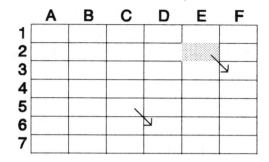

Figure 10.7

This relative addressing applies to cells in all directions, to the right as well as to the left, and also up and down. Let us say that we enter the formula + F3*0.175 in cell E2. The F3 address refers to the cell one to the right and one down from E2. If the formula is copied to cell C5, then it will become + D6*0.175, as D6 is the cell one to the right and one down from C5, as shown in Fig. 10.7.

Absolute addresses

We do not always want to use relative addresses in a formula. We might want always to refer to the same cell in a formula, even when it is copied down a column or across a row. In this case, we will want to make the address *absolute*.

To show that an address is absolute, put '$' signs before the column and row terms. This will fix both the row and the column of the cell: 4*C2 will refer to the entry in cell C2, regardless of which cell the formula is copied to.

Our example above involved adding VAT to prices. At the time of writing, the rate of VAT in the UK is 17.5%, which was why the multiplying factor in the formulas in C1, etc., was 0.175. Suppose that an edict of the European Parliament enforces a uniform rate of 20%. The formula will have to be changed, so that each price is multiplied by $\frac{20}{100} = 0.2$ instead of 0.175. If we had anticipated the possible change, we would have made the formula for calculating VAT take into account the possibility that the rate would change. We would set aside a special cell to contain the VAT rate, say cell F1, and put the number 0.175 into this cell. The entry in cell C1 would then be amended to:

$$+ B1*F1$$

Whenever a new VAT rate is announced, the entry in cell F1 can be altered, and the calculation will change to take account of the new rate.

This would work for cell C1. But when we copied the formula down the column, the address F1 would change to F2, F3, F4, etc., which we wouldn't want. To prevent this change taking place, we need to fix the row, by making it absolute. We want some way to make the row number constant. The entry in cell C1 could be:

$$+B1*\$F\$1$$

The effect of putting the $s in the address is to ensure that this address will not change. Now when we copy the formula down the column, the B1 will change to B2, B3, etc. (we do want this address to change), while the F1 will remain fixed at F1 (we don't want this to change).

Sometimes we will want the column to change but the row to be fixed. In this case, we will put the $ in front of the row number, but not the column letter, i.e. F$1. If we allow the row to change but the column to be fixed, the address would be $F1. If we wanted both row and column to be fixed, the address would be F1.

FURTHER FEATURES

The formula of the previous section was very simple, involving only multiplication. Standard mathematical formulas can all be expressed as spreadsheet formulas, with minor adjustments. We have mentioned that multiplication is shown by '*'. Taking powers is shown by '^', so that 3^2 is written 3^2. Division is shown by /, so $4 \div 5$ is written 4/5. A quadratic formula like $5x^2 + 3x - 5$ would be written as:

$$5*A1^2 + 3*A1 - 5 \qquad \text{(the variable } x \text{ is in cell A1)}$$

A spreadsheet can calculate formulas which are much more complicated than those above.

@functions

Suppose we want to add up a column of numbers. In the example concerning computer equipment, we might want to add up all the prices in the B column. We could do it directly, by putting in cell B7 the formula:

$$+B1+B2+B3+B4+B5+B6$$

This is a very long formula, and we would be liable to make a mistake when typing it in. If we had a column containing a 100 items, it would be time-consuming to type in a formula which directly added them all up. So any spreadsheet will contain a function which adds up all the numbers in a column or in a row. For our example, in cell B7 we could type the function as:

@sum(B1..B6)

This will sum all the numbers in the range from B1 to B6. If we did have a 100 numbers to add up, then the formula can easily be amended to @sum(B1..B100).

The @sum function will also work for rows. Suppose that row 5 contains 12 numbers, in A5 through to L5. To sum these numbers, we type in @sum(A5..L5), and they will be added up automatically.

Note that the distinction between relative and absolute addressing applies to these functions as well as to formulas. For our continuing example, we might want to add up all the VAT for the items. So copy the formula in B7 to C7, and because we have not made the addresses absolute, it will change to:

@sum(C1..C6)

This is exactly what we want. It will sum the entries in the C column, to find the total of the VAT payable.

There are many other @functions available on a spreadsheet. They may include the following:

- *Mathematics functions*
  @sum   (to add up numbers)
  @sqrt   (to find the square root of a number)
- *Financial functions*
  @FV   (this calculates the 'future value' of a regular investment, after a given number of years at a given rate of interest)
- *Statistics functions*
  @avg   (to find the average of a list of numbers)
  @std   (to find the standard deviation of a list of numbers)

An advanced spreadsheet will contain many more of these functions. As you can appreciate, the spreadsheet is a very flexible and powerful tool, in mathematics and statistics as well as in business.

Macros

Spreadsheets were invented so that people could perform intricate calculations without having to program a computer. But a spreadsheet does contain a facility whereby miniature programs can be written and used.

Suppose that there is a sequence of tasks on a spreadsheet that you want to repeat many times. It might be widening a column to accommodate long names. Then instead of having to type in the instructions over and over again, you can automate the procedure by putting them in a *macro*. Then, by operating the macro, which may involve only one or two keys on the keyboard, you can perform all the operations in one go.

The writing of macros is often a fairly intricate procedure, and as it is so close to programming itself, it lies outside the scope of this book.

Three dimensions

As we have described it, the spreadsheet is a two-dimensional thing. It is like an enormous sheet of paper, on which we can move horizontally by changing the column or vertically by changing the row.

Some advanced spreadsheets are three-dimensional, for example Lotus 123 version 3, and Quattro Pro for Windows. When you open the spreadsheet, you have not just a single sheet of paper but a whole book of them. You can move from page to page, as well as from column to column or from row to row. The formulas can work across different pages.

This would be very useful in circumstances in which you want to link together calculations for different years. Suppose you are preparing a survey of the social structure of a disease, and comparing the rate in various countries, across various income groups. The columns could give the country and the rows the income. Different pages of the spreadsheet could give the figures for different years, so that you could follow the course of the disease from year to year, as well as from country to country and up and down the income scale.

Graphics

So far, spreadsheets have been discussed as tools for performing numerical calculations. That is indeed their main task, but they can also produce a pictorial representation of the results.

All the graphs mentioned in Chapter 4 – bar charts, pie charts, line graphs, and so on – can be produced automatically by the computer. Say a car-dealership prepared a spreadsheet showing quarterly sales for two successive years. The steps to produce a bar graph to illustrate this would be as follows:

- Say that you want to draw a bar graph
- Specify the variable that will go along the x-axis (in this case time).
- Specify what you want to display up the y-axis (in this case the number of sales).

You can add labels and headings to the graph. The result might look like that in Fig. 10.8 when it is printed out.

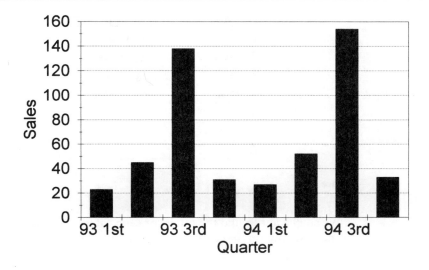

Figure 10.8 Car sales 1993–94

APPLICATIONS

One can make very rapid progress with a spreadsheet. Once you have learned the basics of entering text, numbers and formulas, and have understood how to copy the entries of cells, then you can proceed to do many useful things with spreadsheets without having to learn much else. So we will now give a few applications of spreadsheets to show how useful they can be. The last two of these were used in the writing of this book.

Religious observance at college

This example involves the entry of names, numbers and formulas. It uses copying of entries. It uses the @sum function.

A sociological study is done of the religious observance of the students at a college. The student body is broken down into first, second and third years, and into the groups which attend a place of worship regularly, occasionally or not at all.

A spreadsheet can be used to display the figures. In cells B1, C1 and D1 enter the text 'First year', 'Second year' and 'Third year', respectively. In cells A2, A3 and A4 enter the text 'Regular', 'Occasional' and 'Never', respectively. Now fill in the numbers. Let us suppose that they are as shown as in Fig. 10.9.

	A	B	C	D	E	F
1		1st year	2nd year	3rd year		
2	Regular	53	46	31		
3	Occas.	105	83	69		
4	Never	362	391	420		
5						
6						
7						

Figure 10.9

We shall want to find the totals for each category. To add up the numbers in the first column, in cell B5 we can enter either of:

$$+ B2 + B3 + B4 \quad \text{or} \quad @sum(B2.B4)$$

The total number of first-year students will appear. By copying this formula across to C5 and D5, we can get the total numbers of second- and third-year students.

Similarly, we can find the total numbers of regular attenders, occasional attenders and those who never attend, by finding the row totals. Finally, we can find the total number of students, by adding up either the three column totals or the three row totals.

Sharing expenses

This example involves the use of absolute addresses. Four students – Ron, Ayesha, Tal and Patti – share a house. Every month they write down how much each has paid towards the common expenses of the house, and then share out the cost. None of them is particularly good at arithmetic, even with a calculator, and so they set up a spreadsheet which will work for every month.

In cells B1, C1, D1 and E1 enter the four names. In the next six rows enter the cost of each item bought by each person. Not all the cells need be filled.

First find the total amount spent by Ron, by putting @sum(B2.B7) into cell B8. The totals for the other three can be found by copying this formula across to C8, D8 and E8. The spreadsheet might now look like that depicted in Fig. 10.10.

Now find the total spent by everyone by entering @sum(B8.E8) in cell F8. The *average* expenditure will be the total expenditure divided by the number of people in the house, so in F9 enter the formula $+ F8/4$.

Ron has spent more than the average, so he should be paid the difference between what he spent and the average. In B9 enter a formula to obtain

Cell: D8 @SUM(D2.D7)

	A	B	C	D	E	F
1		Ron	Ayesha	Tal	Patti	
2		7.5	5	3.1	9.31	
3		32.85	12.3	6.3		
4		43.12	5.3	12.15		
5		6.35				
6						
7						
8		89.82	22.6	21.55	9.31	
9						

Figure 10.10

this. We shall be copying this formula across to the other columns, and the average expenditure remains the same for all four people. So we must ensure that the address holding the average expenditure is made absolute. The formula to enter in B9 is:

$$+B8 - \$F9$$

Copy this formula across, and we shall see how much everyone is owed, or – if the sum is negative – owes.

Correlation coefficient

This example uses more complicated formulas, and the @sum and @sqrt functions. It involves copying more than one cell.

In Chapter 4, we defined the correlation coefficient between two variables, which shows how closely they are connected to each other. The actual calculation of the coefficient is complicated, and it is easy to make a mistake. With a spreadsheet, you can enter the figures and all the calculation is done automatically for you.

Table 6.1 (p.86) gives a collection of 20 values of x and y. From these values we have to calculate x^2, y^2 and xy. We then have to sum all the values.

1. Leave the first row for the headings. Down the A column write the x-values. Down the B column write the y-values.
2. The C column will contain the values of x^2. So in C2 enter $+A2^2$. Do not copy this to the rest of the column yet, as we will save time by doing all the copying in one go.

3. The D column will contain the values of y^2. So in D2 enter $+$B2$^\wedge$2.
4. The E column will contain the values of xy. So in E2 enter $+$A2*B2.

Now we can do the copying. The steps are:

- Tell the program you want to copy.
- Select the cells to copy *from* (in this case it is C2.E2).
- Select the cells to copy *to* (in this case it is C3.E21).

You should find that the columns contain the functions as required.

The column totals must now be found. At the bottom of the x-column, in A22, enter the formula:

$$@\text{sum(A2..A21)}$$

You will now see 71 appear at the bottom of the column. Copy this across to B22, C22, D22 and E22. All the columns have now been totalled.

From these values we can find the correlation coefficient. You can use the spreadsheet itself to calculate it. You could type in one single formula, or you could do it in stages. Doing it by stages, in F1 enter the top line of the formula, corresponding to $n\Sigma xy - \Sigma x\Sigma y$. This will be:

$$20*\text{E22} - \text{A22}*\text{B22}$$

In F2 and F3 enter the two expressions inside the square root sign, $n\Sigma x^2 - (\Sigma x)^2$ and $n\Sigma y^2 - (\Sigma y)^2$. The formulas are:

$$20*\text{C22} - \text{A22}^\wedge 2 \quad \text{and} \quad 20*\text{D22} - \text{B22}^\wedge 2$$

The bottom row of the expression is the square root of these two expressions. So in F4 enter:

$$@\text{sqrt(F2*F3)}$$

Finally, we divide the top by the bottom. In F5 enter:

$$+\text{F1/F4}$$

The number 0.297 will appear. This is the correlation coefficient.

Note: if you have an advanced word-processor, it is possible to take the numbers from the spreadsheet and put them directly into the text. So this saves you having to type in all the numbers, and you eliminate the risk of typing errors.

Contingency table

This example makes more advanced use of absolute addresses. It is quite tricky, and if you can understand it, then you have mastered the basic use of a spreadsheet.

On pp. 92–4 we solved a problem involving a contingency table. It involved comparing the reading abilities of pupils who had been taught by different methods. All the arithmetical calculations can be done on a spreadsheet.

First, set up the row and column headings as shown on p. 92. Enter the numerical data of the observed frequencies. This is one thing the computer cannot do for you. The result should be as on p. 92.

First we want the row and column totals. So in E2 enter @sum(B2..D2). You will see the entry change to the sum of the numbers in the first row. Copy this formula down to E3, E4, E5. Similarly, in B5 enter @sum(B2..B4). You will see the entry change to the sum of the numbers in the first column. Copy this formula across to C5, D5.

You want this whole table to be copied, in order to find the expected frequencies. So tell the computer that you want to copy. The range you are copying from is A1..E5, and the range you are copying to is say A7..E11.

This will still have the observed frequencies as entries. The expected frequencies are found by multiplying the row and column totals of the observed frequencies, and then dividing by the total of all the frequencies.

To find the expected frequency of Good L&S pupils, we will multiply the entries in the top row and left column, E2 and B5. The expected frequency of bad LE pupils will involve multiplying E4 and D5. Comparing these two, we see that the column of the first term and the row of the second term have stayed fixed. So we want to make these absolute. The formula will involve:

$$\$E2*B\$5$$

We want to divide by the grand total, which is in E5. But we will be copying this formula, and though we want the rows and columns to change we don't want the grand total to change. So the grand total reference will be absolute for both row and column. So in cell B8 enter the formula:

$$+\$E2*B\$5/\$E\$5$$

This should now be 29.75. Copy the formula in B8 to the whole block B8..D10, and the table of expected frequencies appears. You have a check, as these figures should match the ones on p. 93

To work out the value of χ^2, we have to find the differences between the tables, square the differences, divide by the expected frequencies, and add up. In cell B14 put the formula involving the top left entries in the tables, which is:

$$((B2 - B8)\wedge 2)/B8$$

Copy this formula to the block B14..E16.

Finally, we need to add all these up. In cell B20 put @sum(B14..E16). The correct value of 30.88 will appear.

Statistical packages

The last two examples involved complicated statistical formulas. To manage the second one, in particular, required patience and a thorough understanding of the workings of a spreadsheet. There are programs, similar to spreadsheets, which set up the statistical calculations for you. We shall discuss one of these in Chapter 12.

11   Databases

Most people probably think of a computer as a device for handling vast quantities of information. This is largely true; though computers are used to perform mathematical calculations, and in the home they are used to play games and write letters, the majority of commercial work with computers involves dealing with large amounts of data.

The program you are most likely to use to handle data is called a *Database Management System*. This is often abbreviated to *Database*, though strictly this word should apply to the collection of data, not the means of organizing it.

The other two applications of computers that we have dealt with, word-processing and spreadsheets, can be learned fairly quickly. By and large, this is because within a few minutes of starting up these programs you can experiment with them, and correct your mistakes as you go along. It is much harder to learn to use a database efficiently, as there is not much you can do with it until you have acquired considerable understanding of how it works and what it can do. You also have to enter a large amount of data before you can do anything useful.

Another difficulty with databases is the lack of uniformity in the words used and the methods of operation. A database designed for a large computer or a network may have different terminology to one used in an isolated PC. In this chapter, we shall describe a database for a PC.

The closest non-computer analogy of a database is a card-index. Up until a few years ago, the cataloguing of library books was done by a cabinet containing a card for each book, containing the necessary information about it. Nowadays, libraries have computerized their catalogues, so that the function of those cabinets containing thousands of cards has been taken over by a database.

RECORDS AND FIELDS

How do you organize your data? If you are undertaking a research project, you will accumulate a great mass of facts, which must be organized in some way if you are to make any sense out of them. Somehow you must be able to link together bits of information with common properties.

Consider the library card-index mentioned above. Each card refers to a given book, and will contain the following data:

- Title
- Name of author
- Date of publication
- Reference number

Each of these classifications is called a *field*. They will appear on each of the cards.

The cards themselves are called *records*. So the catalogue of a library has organized the information about its books into several thousand records, one per book, each of which contains an entry under the given fields: title, name of author, date of publication, reference number.

A database follows this pattern. The fields are the headings under which we classify the information. The records provide the information about each individual item.

Another example is a doctor's patient list. There will be a record for each patient. The fields under which the patient will be classified might include the following:

- Reference number
- Surname
- First names
- Sex
- Address
- Telephone number
- Date of birth

You can think of the database as a huge table, with the columns corresponding to the fields, and the rows to the records. Part of the doctor's database might look like the following:

Reference number	Surname	First names	Sex	Address
123734	Jones	John Eric	M	13 Acacia Gardens
684790	Worple	Fred	M	47 Gasworks Terrace
790476	D'Avignon	Daphne	F	17 Posh Villas

and so on.

There are many tasks for which a database is appropriate. Throughout this chapter, we shall use the following examples, as well as the ones above.

- *Magazine subscribers.* A database could be used to keep information of the subscribers to a magazine. The fields will include name, address as above, and also the date at which the subscription should be renewed.

- *Books written.* An author of crime fiction might want to keep track of all her books and the royalties she has received from them. The fields of the database will include title, publisher, date of publication, total sales, and so on.
- *Historical Records.* Suppose you are doing a thesis on crime in the West Riding in the eighteenth century. You may find it convenient to keep the information on a database, with fields for: name of prisoner, date when tried, age, sex, occupation, court where tried.

SETTING UP A DATABASE

When you set up a database, you have to state what the fields are, what sort of information they will hold, and how large they must be. When you tell the computer that you wish to open a new database, the screen will be like a form on which you enter the required information.

The information is classified into different groups, as you will want to do different things to the name of a person, his date of birth or his annual income. When you set up the fields, you will be asked what sort of information it will contain. The groups might be:

- *Alphanumeric*: This is for storing actual words, such as names or addresses. There could be numbers in an address, so we are not restricted to letters. But we will not be able to perform any arithmetic on the numbers.
- *Numerical*: This will store an actual number, on which you might want to perform arithmetic.
- *Date*: This might record the date of birth of a person, or the date of a purchase.

When you declare the size of each field, you must allow for the greatest possible length that is likely to arise. For the example of the doctor's patient list, one field might be called 'Surname'. The information will be alphanumeric. It is very unlikely that anyone's surname will be longer than 20 letters and so you allow 20 letters for this field.

You will allow perhaps 50 characters for first names and 50 for address. Both of these will also be alphanumeric. The sex can be recorded by just one letter, M or F. There is a special category for dates, as they are so common in databases, and this is how you will store the date of birth.

These categories can be changed, or added to, or deleted. You can also extend the length allotted to them, if for example a patient with an abnormally long surname appears.

- *Memo fields*: Often you will want to enter information in a record of variable length. You might want to enter a couple of sentences of comments. A memo field will set aside space for this.

Entering records

Once you have decided on the fields, you can enter the records. For each record you will be prompted to give the information that should appear under each field. Again, these entries can be changed, for example if a patient changes address, or if information has been entered wrongly.

It should be apparent why databases are so complicated to learn. So much work has to be done – deciding upon the fields and entering all the data – before anything sensible can be done with them.

Sorting

If a card-index contains a large number of cards, it is difficult to find a particular card unless they are arranged in some particular way. For the library example above, there are several ways we could order the cards for the books:

● Alphabetically by author
● Alphabetically by title
● Chronologically by date of publication
● Numerically by reference number

If the cards were arranged in one particular order, it would be an enormous labour physically to rearrange them in another order. But if the book information is electronically coded on a database, then it is straightforward to change the order. You just give the instructions, and the computer does all the hard work.

Recall that the classifications are called fields. Any of the fields can be used to order the records. You could decide to order the records under the Name field or the Date field, and so on.

Often there will be several records with the same entry in a field. Among magazine subscribers, for example, there may be several people with the same surname. We need a 'tie-breaker' to distinguish between these people. So all the people with surname Smith, for example, will themselves be sorted by first name.

The first field under which records are sorted is the *primary* field. The second field for sorting records with identical entries in the primary field is the *secondary* field. And so on. If there are many John Smiths, then it may be necessary to have a tertiary field.

Key fields

When records are entered into a database, unless you say otherwise, they are added to the end of the list. This may not be what you want. You might want the new records to appear in the correct alphabetic position. It would be a nuisance to sort the whole database every time you entered a new record, and so you can arrange it so they are slotted into their correct position. Designate a field as a *key* field, and new records will automatically be put in the right place. As above, you may have several records with the same entry in the key field, and so you can designate secondary or even tertiary key fields.

Let us take the example of a library catalogue. The primary key field will be the name of the author. As an author may write many different books, the secondary keyfield will be the title of the book. It is very unlikely that an author will write two books with the same title, so a tertiary keyfield is not needed.

QUERIES

To be useful, a database contains hundreds or maybe thousands of records. There are many hours of work involved in typing all the details for each record. You want to make full use of that labour, by doing more than could be done by a simple card file. You will want to extract information from the database quickly and automatically. This is done by *queries*.

The result of a query is to pick out and display on the screen those records which obey certain conditions. This might be a single record – the query could just pick out for example the record with a certain reference number. The result might be a whole group of records – for the library catalogue example, you could pick out all the books written by a certain author. You can combine conditions; the result of a query could be to display all the books written by a certain author before a certain date. We could have a more complicated combination. Suppose an author writes under two names. We could search for all the books written under either name, which are neither fiction nor poetry.

The query could contain mathematical conditions. The result of a query might be to alter the records in a database. Below are some examples of queries.

1. *Doctor's patient list*. The result of a query might be to list all the female patients over 70. The doctor might want to offer all of these patients a certain form of preventative medicine.

2. *Magazine subscriber list*. The result of a query might be to list all the subscribers whose subscription was more than one month overdue. This query uses arithmetic on dates – in this case, the date at which the subscription ran out. The query can be arranged so that it deletes from the database all the records it has listed – so that the people with overdue subscriptions no longer receive the magazine.

3. *Books written.* An author might want to know how many of her books have sold more than a certain number of copies. A query can handle a numerical condition like this. One of the fields of the database registered the number of books sold, and the query can pick out the records whose entry in this field exceeds the number.

4. *Historical records.* The student who is writing a thesis about crime in the West Riding could find who, under 18 years of age, were tried between 1760 and 1780. This might be a useful line of enquiry if she was concerned about whether there had been an increase in the number of young offenders over this period.

5. *Saving queries.* It may take a while to set up a query and make sure that it works properly. If the query is going to be used again, then it makes sense to save it. In our magazine example, the procedure of finding out which subscribers are overdue will have to be done regularly, every month perhaps. So this query will be run every month. If the query is saved, then it can be called up and re-used.

REPORTS

The queries of the previous section display on the screen the records which satisfy certain conditions. The results of a *report* will be printed.

The simplest report will just print out the entire database: all the records, under all the fields. Often you will want to show only part of the database, those records which satisfy certain conditions, and only some of the fields. This sort of report is equivalent to printing out the result of a query.

You can also put text in a report – perhaps a heading to explain what the records have in common. You can also print out a summary at the end – perhaps a total based on the selected records.

1. *Books written.* Our author will want to have a record of how much money she has earned from royalties. She will need to print out, and send to the tax authorities, a list of all her titles and how much she has made from each of them in the tax year. There will be a total at the bottom which adds up all her earnings.

2. *Historical records.* The researcher might want a complete record of trials of defendants under 18 at Gomersal Assizes between 1760 and 1780. This will be printed out as a list giving particulars in all the fields set up: name, age, sex, occupation.

3. *Mail merge.* Everyone is familiar with this use of databases. When you receive unsolicited letters, about prize draws or special offers, they come with a standard text but with your name and address. Obviously they are not

typed individually for each recipient. They are sent to a large number of people who happen to be on a mailing-list database.

The basic text is written. This is the same for all the people to whom the letter is sent. Special coding is put in the letter, to show where your address should go, where your name should go, and so on. Instructions are given for who should receive the letter – perhaps only people within a certain age range, or living in a certain area. Then the computer can print out the letter for all the people on the database who satisfy the given conditions, and customize the letters with the individual name and address.

4. *Printing labels*. One very common use of database is printing out address labels. The staff of the magazine will post it to all the subscribers, using labels printed out from the database. Indeed, many databases are used for little else.

Saving reports

As with queries, a report might be used over and over again. You will be able to save a report, so that you do not need to set it up anew every time it is used. The author who prints out the total amount of money she has received from royalties will need to repeat the process every year, so she will save this report for future use.

FORMS

When you enter new records into the database, or amend old ones, the default arrangement is for you to see the information as a large table with rows for the records and columns for the fields. This may not always be convenient – if there are many fields, for example, they will not all fit onto the screen. With a different *form* you can make data entry and amendment easier.

A form for data entry would typically show only one record on the screen. There would be a space for each field, which can then be filled in. A form for entering new subscribers to the magazine might look like the following:

- Name
- Address
- Postcode
- Expiry of subscription

Whoever is filling in the details does not have to be an expert with computers. All that is required is to type in the name, address, and so on at the relevant places.

RELATIONAL DATABASES

The database which is closest to an electronic version of a card-file is called a *flat file* database. It is the simplest form of database. Its main limitation is that there is a fixed number of fields under which each record is classified.

Some records might require a large amount of information, and some only a small amount. We would not want to arrange the database so that each record had enough space to accommodate the largest possible amount of information. This would be extremely wasteful of space, and would be completely impracticable if there were thousands of records. Furthermore, however much space is set aside for information, a special case may come along which requires more, and then the whole database will have to be redesigned.

Consider the example of the doctor's patient list. The record for each patient will contain information about name, address, sex, date of birth, and so on. Note there is nothing medical about any of these fields. The doctor will also want to keep track of the visits the patient makes to the surgery, and of the various diseases contracted throughout the patient's lifetime.

There is wide variation in the number of times people visit their doctor. Some people only visit once every few years, for example when they have come down with glandular fever. Other people, very sickly or very hypochondriac, visit their doctor frequently. There will be a corresponding difference in the amount of information the doctor will need to keep about the patient.

Such a situation can be resolved with a *relational* database. The doctor's database will have several files. We have already described one of them, with fields containing the basic information about name, date of birth, and so on. Then there will be further files recording all the visits to the surgery, or referrals to the local hospital. The files are linked, so that information can be passed between them. We can find out how many times Mr Jones has visited the surgery, or we can pick out all the women over 35 who have ever complained about back pain.

In all cases, the two related files must have a field in common, through which they are linked. The patient file and the hospital visit file will be linked by having one field in common, perhaps the patient's reference number. Here are some other examples:

1. *Magazine subscribers*. The database for this might have no use other than to keep track of the subscriptions to the magazine, in which case it would just be a flat file database. If the magazine was the journal of a learned society, then there might be a lot of additional information that could be kept. The subscribers might themselves be contributors to the journal, in which case the database could include a second file, containing data about the articles they had written. There might be special subscription rates for those who had written at least two articles for the journal. When the

subscription reminder is sent out, those who were entitled to a reduction could be found by reference to the second file in the database.

2. *Books written.* Our author will want to keep track of how many copies of each book have been sold and how much she made from them. Every six months she will get royalty statements from her publisher, giving this information and the royalty cheque. If the details of the sales were to be put on the records of the original database, an enormous amount of space would have to be set aside. Some of her books, perhaps, have continued selling for decades after they were written. Some of her books were less successful, and did not sell after the first year. But enough space would have to be set aside on the records of these unpopular books to accommodate decades of sales.

One answer is for her to construct a second file in her database, to contain the records of the sales. The fields of this second file will be:

- Title
- Date of payment
- Price
- Sales
- Amount received

If she is on a commission rate of 10%, then the number in the last field is calculated automatically from the two previous fields. It is given by:

$$\text{Amount received} = \text{Price} \times \text{Sales} \times 0.1$$

Then every six months, when she receives a royalty statement, she can update this second file. She might enter:

Blood at the Hotel Bristol	2/10/94	£5.99	435	£260.56
The Cheltenham Corpse	2/10/94	£6.45	602	£388.29
Strike Me Pink	2/10/94	£6.95	1048	£728.36

Note that the two files share a field in common, that of the title. Entry of information into the second file will alter the first one – the total sales will be upgraded to take account of her latest royalty statement.

She can make a query which requires information from both files. She could find out which books have made more than £10,000 for her since a certain date.

3. *Historical records.* The researcher will, as we have seen, keep records on individuals brought before the courts. She also has a file on court proceedings. This file has the following fields: court, date of trial, prisoner, offence, verdict, sentence. As you can see, there are three fields common to the two files: prisoner, court and date of trial. Our researcher will be able to make a query which requires information from both files. For example, she may wish to find out how many women weavers were transported to Australia between 1770 and 1790.

OTHER FACILITIES

Database Management Systems are often huge programs. They may include facilities for programming, for drawing tables and graphs based on the data in the database, for exchanging information with other application programs like spreadsheets, and so on. These other facilities lie outside the scope of this book.

DATABASES, PRIVACY AND THE LAW

Computerized databases can contain enormous amounts of information in a very small space. Much of the information they hold is confidential. A timeshare firm might be interested in gaining information about the income or credit rating of people in a particular town. If such information is available on electronic databases, then it might be tempting to get hold of it as a preliminary to a sales campaign. There are various ways of consulting electronic databases, such as by modem or through a network. Some people are authorized to gain access to a particular database, but unauthorized people might be able to gain access by bribery or by hacking into someone else's network.

It is not difficult to see that records can fall into the wrong hands and that the information stored on databases might be used to help someone at the expense of someone else. For example, an insurance company might wish to check a patient's medical records to see if he is a good risk. Worse still, an unscrupulous individual employee of the insurance company might then go on to sell this information or even use it to blackmail the doctor's patient.

Modern computer and communications technology has the potential to allow state agencies, commercial companies or unscrupulous people to gain information that will help them to harm the interests of others by gaining access to electronic databases. It is not even necessary to leave the office in order to gain access to the information; a few keystrokes and mouse clicks might be enough. In order to protect the individual, the Data Protection Act 1988 allows everyone the right to see what information is being held on them. It also requires those who hold data on individuals to register the type of information they hold and the purposes for which they hold it.

This could be relevant to you if, for example, you were holding information about living individuals for use in your dissertation. If you are holding data on individual people, you should ensure that you are complying with the law, by making that information available to them should they request it. The law also requires you to take measures to ensure that only authorized individuals have access to such data.

The Data Protection Act provides guidelines to help you comply with the law in holding information on a database:

1. You must register the nature of the information which you hold and the purposes for which you are holding it with your employer (in this case, your college or university).
2. You must obtain and process your data in a fair and lawful manner.
3. You must only use the data for the purposes specified in your register.
4. You should only hold data which are adequate, relevant and not excessive for your stated purposes.
5. You should ensure that personal data are adequate and up to date.
6. You should hold data for no longer than is necessary.
7. You should allow individuals named in your database access to information concerning them and, if appropriate, correct or erase it.
8. You should make sure that your data are secure and take proper steps to prevent unauthorized access.

Databases, like other aspects of computer technology, provide such enormous potential power for their users that there must be rules to ensure that that power is not misused.

12   Analysing your own data using a statistical package

In this chapter, we are going to show you how the techniques and materials that we have described in previous chapters can be put to use in planning and carrying out your own research. It is now very common for third-year students on arts and social science courses to have to produce a dissertation based upon a small-scale piece of research planned and carried out by themselves. Many students do not feel that they have either the confidence or the skill to carry out research which requires the use of mathematical and computational techniques. Because of this, they may exclude themselves from working on a range of interesting projects. It is hoped that, after reading this chapter, you will feel more confident about undertaking such work yourself.

The approach that we adopt is to describe a piece of research (which is very loosely based on one carried out by one of the authors) from beginning to end, showing how mathematical and computational techniques were used along the way. We have changed the names and greatly simplified the whole scheme, but in principle the project described here has the same structure as the one carried out. Although this research was carried out full-time by academic researchers, it is quite similar to the kind of work that you could undertake as part of a third-year project or Master's dissertation. The research described here was carried out on an island in the West Indies, rather than in the UK.

THE RESEARCH PROJECT

Background

There is a view among educators, both in Britain and in the West Indies, that some children of West Indian origin experience difficulties in learning to write because their spoken dialect, Creole, is quite different from the standard English that they are taught to write in. One can tell that their difficulties with writing have this origin, it is argued, because constructions that are common in speech but which are considered 'ungrammatical' in written standard English, can be commonly found in the written work of the children. The presence of these features, it is claimed, shows that the children have difficulties learning to write in standard English, which are *caused* by the fact that they speak in Creole. This theory is commonly known as the *Creole interference hypothesis* and was the *research hypothesis* for this project (see Chapter 5). The *null hypothesis* was that Creole interference has *no* effect on the quality of the children's writing.

The researchers wished to test this theory by looking at a sample of children's written work and checking for features that one would expect to find if the Creole interference hypothesis were true. If these features were present and were associated with lower quality written work, then the Creole interference hypothesis would receive some support. It would not be *proved* for reasons that we examined in Chapter 5 of this book. On the other hand, if the errors could not be found, or, if they were found and yet were not significantly associated with poorer quality written work, then the Creole interference hypothesis would not be supported.

The island of St. Eustace, where this particular work was carried out, is about 200 square miles in area and has a population of about 150,000 people. The plan for the research was to take a sample of the work of 150 eleven-year-old children around the island, to mark it for quality, and then to analyse it for signs of features that could plausibly be attributed to Creole interference. The idea was to take a sample of schools in both rural and urban areas, so that all sections of the population of 11-year-olds would have an equal chance of being included in the study. It was decided to visit the classes of 11-year-olds in five schools selected at random. All the children were given identical tasks to be carried out in identical conditions. Each child had to complete a story that was begun for them. They also had to write a letter of complaint to a shopkeeper. In all, 300 scripts were collected from 150 children in five different classes. All the scripts were marked three times by the two researchers and by a teacher. The *mean* of the three marks was used for the purposes of analysis.

Marking the scripts

The scripts were marked as follows. First, they were marked for an overall impression of quality on a scale of 1 (low) to 5 (high). When the scripts had been marked for impression of quality, they were subjected to an analysis which considered five categories of possible Creole interference features. These features are listed in Table 12.1.

Some words of explanation of these features are as follows.

[1] *Use of imperfect for perfect (IFP).* This refers to when a writer uses the imperfect rather than the perfect when the latter would be more appropriate. For example:

> I drank the juice and it was not tasting good.

Table 12.1   Possible Creole features of scripts

[1] Use of imperfect for perfect (IFP)
[2] Inappropriate shift of tense in sentence (ISTIS)
[3] Hypercorrection (HYP)
[4] Incorrect use of preposition (IUP)
[5] Loans (L)

[2] *Inappropriate shift of tense in sentence (ISTIS).* This occurs when the tense changes in a sentence when it should not. For example:

> I bought a tin of orange juice yesterday and when I drink it, it tastes sour.

In this example, which is an account of what *happened*, you can see that the verb 'bought' is in the past, but 'drink' and 'taste' are in the present.

[3] *Hypercorrection (HYP).* This refers to a situation where an irregular word form is treated as a regular form as in 'I runned' rather than 'I ran'. For example:

> When I left your shop, I runned all the way home because I felt sick.

[4] *Incorrect use of preposition (IUP).* This happens when the writer uses an incorrect preposition. For example:

> I took the bottle by him   *rather than*   I took the bottle from him.

[5] *Loans (L).* These occur when a word in the Creole dialect is used instead of the standard English form. For example:

> I hurt my pied   *rather than*   I hurt my foot.

In this case, the French-based word 'pied' is 'on loan' from Creole and has been incorporated into an English sentence.

Each of the 300 scripts was checked for features in the categories indicated in Table 12.1. These were noted down on paper and the number of scripts with features in each category was also noted. When this was done, the information was transferred onto the sheet displayed in Table 12.2.

This sheet is set out in such a way that all a researcher need do is ring the appropriate number in order to record the information:

I   If impression marker A gave a script a score of 3, for example, then 3 was ringed in this row.
II   The school from which the script came was indicated in this row.
III   If a script had 3 errors in the category 'incorrect use of preposition', then under [4], the number 3 was ringed, and so on.

Table 12.2 Coding frame for script analysis.

Script Code _____
I   Impression mark   *Marker A*: 1 2 3 4 5   *Marker B*: 1 2 3 4 5
                        Marker C: 1 2 3 4 5   *Overall*:   1 2 3 4 5

II   1..2..3..4..5. (school)

III [1] 1 2 3 4 5   [2] 1 2 3 4 5   [3] 1 2 3 4 5
     [4] 1 2 3 4 5   [5] 1 2 3 4 5   (Creole interference features)

The following is a typical script. Perhaps you would like to give an overall impression mark, and see if you can spot any of the Creole interference features mentioned above.

Dear shopkeeper,

The juice I purchase at your shop was expired. When I was drinking the jus it made me sick. So I poured the juice in a glass and seed that it was brown. I will bring the juice to get it change or get my money back.

The researchers marked it as follows, and the corresponding record sheet was as shown in Table 12.3. There is an example of ISTIS in the first sentence ('I purchase' instead of 'I purchased'). In the second sentence, there is an example of the imperfect used for the past ('I was drinking' for 'I drank'). In the the third sentence, there is an example of hypercorrection ('I seed' for 'I saw') and the incorrect use of a preposition ('in' for 'into'). In the final sentence, there is another example of ISTIS ('to get it change' instead of 'to get it changed'). The overall impression mark given was 3, which is the mean of 4, 3 and 2, which the three markers gave to the script.

Table 12.3 Completed record sheet

Script Code _____
I   Impression mark   *Marker A*: 1 2 3 ④ 5   *Marker B*: 1 2 ③ 4 5
                        Marker C: 1 ② 3 4 5   *Overall*: 1 2 ③ 4 5

II   1..2..③..4..5 (school)

III [1] ① 2 3 4 5   [2] 1 ② 3 4 5   [3] ① 2 3 4 5
     [4] ① 2 3 4 5   [5] 1 2 3 4 5   (Creole interference features)

When all 300 scripts were coded in this way, it was possible to give the results to the computer. The second stage of the project could begin.

ANALYSING DATA ON THE COMPUTER

The program used in this case was SPSS Windows, which is derived from a mainframe program called SPSS (Statistical Package for the Social Sciences). In some ways, SPSS is similar to the spreadsheets that were discussed in Chapter 10. Data are entered on the same kind of grid that is used on a spreadsheet. SPSS provides a large battery of statistical tests which can be applied to the data that you have logged in, and it can compute these statistics for your data with great speed. It can also show the analysis graphically or in the form of charts.

Entering data

When you have loaded up SPSS Windows, it is now possible to enter your data. You tell the computer that this is the task you want to do by selecting 'Data Editor' and then 'Newdata'. You have, in front of you, a grid like a spreadsheet grid, which is organized into rows and columns. The situation is rather like that of the databases in Chapter 11, in which the information was organized into records and fields.

The rows are *cases* and the columns are *variables*. The cases are the particular sheets of data that were created and which are displayed in Table 12.2. The variables are the impression mark awarded to the script and the different types of feature that were identified and named. The place where rows and columns intersect is called the *cell*. Each cell represents a particular case of a particular variable. Thus if case 1 has an impression mark of 1, then the first cell will have the number 1 entered into it. If case 4 contained two occurrences of feature [1] (i.e. IFP), then the second cell in the fourth row will contain the number 2.

You can either enter the data case by case or variable by variable. If we suppose you have the sheets in a pile in front of you, then it would be easier to enter the data case by case, by doing each sheet in turn and then setting it aside and moving on to the next one. This means that for each case you will move along the rows until you have filled in all the data. Where there is no error of a particular kind on a sheet, then we put a score of zero in the appropriate cell.

At present, the variables are identified by number, such as var00001 for the first column, var00002 for the second column, and so on. You can continue with these numbers, but it might help if the variables have names so that you can remember what they mean. The first column registers the impression mark of the scripts, so you can call it IMPMARK. You could name the variables corresponding to the errors similarly.

After the information has been entered, the first part of the table might look like that shown in Fig. 12.1.

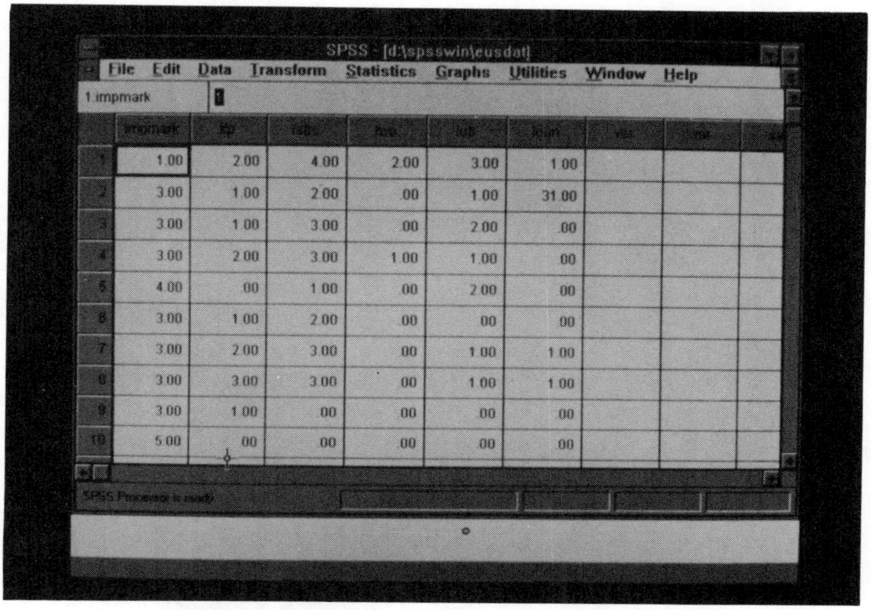

Figure 12.1

Analysing the data

It has taken a great deal of time and effort to enter all the data. From now on, though, nearly all the hard work is done automatically. As well as relieving you of the tedious work of calculation, the program will be more accurate than any human being could hope to be.

The first statistical thing that most researchers do is to get descriptive data giving the frequencies and percentages of cases according to each variable. If you look at the illustration of the screen in Fig. 12.1, you will see that one of the options is 'Statistics'. Select this as the thing to do next, and then select 'Frequencies'. This will allow you to look at all the impression marks and gain frequencies and percentages of each mark. It will also calculate the frequencies and percentages of features in each of the categories. You can choose to look at only some of the cases or variables, or at all of them.Table 12.4 gives the frequencies and percentages corresponding to the possible impression marks.

The researchers can now get an idea of the distribution of the impression marks. This can also be put into pictorial form, by means of a pie chart or bar chart. Again, these can be printed out automatically. Figure 12.2 is a pie chart corresponding to Table 12.4.

Just by looking at Table 12.4 and Fig. 12.2, we can make the observation that the marks are reasonably spread, with more in the middle bands than

Table 12.4   Frequency of impression marks (1 = low, 5 = high) in five schools in St. Eustace

Impression mark	Frequency	Percentage
1	39	13
2	75	25
3	108	16
4	48	16
5	30	10

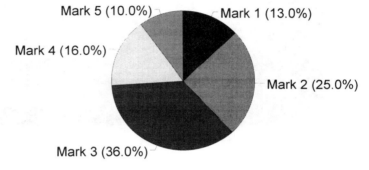

Figure 12.2   Frequency of marks

in the outer two. The marks are also reasonably symmetrical about the middle. Of course, this is a function of the marking criteria as well as of the quality of the scripts.

The program was also able to print out the percentage frequencies of the five Creole interference features, as shown in Table 12.5. The table shows the frequencies of features that previous research assumed to be due to Creole interference. A striking feature of Table 12.5 is that it suggests that the occurrence of some of the features is quite frequent. Given this fact, it is now possible to take the next step and investigate whether or not the presence of the Creole features has an effect on impression marks.

Table 12.5   Possible Creole features of scripts: Percentage of scripts containing errors in each category

Category	%
[1] Use of imperfect for perfect (IFP)	15.5
[2] Inappropriate shift of tense in sentence (ISTIS)	24.7
[3] Hypercorrection (HYP)	11.7
[4] Incorrect use of preposition (IUP)	16.7
[5] Loans (L)	10.6

Significance of results

The next step that the researchers took was to enquire whether or not scripts with low impression marks were associated with high levels in the Creole interference categories. They had to make sure that the results they obtained were not merely due to chance, but were statistically significant.

In Chapter 6, we did several significance tests. The one we shall use here is the χ^2-test. This test, if you recall, compares the frequencies that have been found (the *observed* frequencies) with the frequencies that would be expected if there were no connection between the quantities being investigated (the *expected* frequencies). When we met this in Chapter 6, there was a lot of work needed before a result was obtained. We had to put the observed data into a table, calculate another table for the expected frequencies, and then work out a complicated formula comparing the two. We then had to look up the result in a table of the χ^2-distribution, to see whether or not it was significant.

Even when we used a computer to help us, as in Chapter 10, there was a great deal of hard work involved in making sure the spreadsheet formulas did their job properly. However, with a dedicated statistics package like SPSS, all the processes can be automated.

First, the data are sorted out into tables. The technique employed to do this is known as *cross-tabulation*. All the scripts with features in category III were sorted into their impression mark bands. SPSS will carry out these operations very easily and rapidly. On the 'Statistics' menu, select 'Cross-tabulation'.

We are doing a χ^2-test, so we must decide which properties we are going to compare. Let us try comparing the overall impression mark with the occurrence of the feature ISTIS. The result is shown in Table 12.6. We note that the percentage of scripts with the feature is higher in the lower mark bands than in the higher ones. But is it significantly so?

This test will show whether or not there is any significant connection between the mark and the error frequency. If ISTIS had no effect on script quality whatsoever, one would expect that there would be a proportionate

Table 12.6   Cross-tabulation of impression mark with ISTIS

Impression mark	ISTIS frequency	% of scripts with feature
1	12	30.1
2	20	26.7
3	28	26.0
4	10	20.8
5	4	13.3

distribution of errors at each marking band level, that is, the proportion of scripts with the error at each level would be the same.

If we were doing this by hand, we would apply a χ^2-test to the observed frequencies in Table 12.7. The first row gives the number of scripts in each impression mark band which contains one or more example of this feature, the second row the number of scripts without this feature. We would have to calculate the corresponding table for expected frequencies, and then work out the formula for χ^2. We would then look up the value found to see whether or not it is significant.

Table 12.7   Observed frequencies

| | Impression mark | | | | |
	1	*2*	*3*	*4*	*5*
ISTIS frequency	12	20	28	10	4
Non-ISTIS frequency	27	55	80	38	26

SPSS does all these tasks for us automatically. It gives the approximate value of χ^2 significance as 0.48. This means that if the null hypothesis were true, that there is no connection between the impression mark and the frequency of ISTIS, there would be a chance of 0.48 of obtaining these results. If, as usual, we are performing tests at a significance level of 5%, then this result is not significant.

A cross-tabulation was also carried out with variable [3], Incorrect Use of Preposition and Overall Impression Mark. The results are shown in Table 12.8. These results are even less significant than those for ISTIS. We certainly cannot conclude that there is a definite connection between occurrence of this Creole feature and the impression mark.

Table 12.8   Cross-tabulation of impression mark with IUP

Impression mark	Frequency of scripts in each category
1	8
2	12
3	20
4	8
5	2

Approximate significance of $\chi^2 = 0.58$.

Grouping data

So far, we have had little success in showing a significant connection between individual errors and impression mark. We would like to consider all the errors together. SPSS also allows you to group data and then to cross-tabulate it. This means that all the feature categories were lumped together and broken down by impression mark. This was a useful thing to do in order to establish whether or not the Creole features *as a whole* had any effect on impression marks. Once again, the null hypothesis was that there would be no association. Table 12.9 gives the frequencies of scripts which had one or more of the features.

Table 12.9 Cross-tabulation of impression mark with total Creole syntactic features

1	30
2	40
3	58
4	20
5	10

Approximate significance of $\chi^2 = 0.003$.

Now this result is significant. By considering all the features together, we have an association with the impression mark which would be very unlikely to occur by chance if the null hypothesis were true. As we can see, the chance is less than 5%.

Conclusion

The conclusion of this part of the St. Eustace research was as follows. The research hypothesis was that difficulties with written expression are associated with the prevalence of Creole interference features. The difficulties were associated with scripts having a low impression mark.

Though none of the individual features showed a significant association with the impression mark, when they were lumped together they did show a significant association. We can therefore conclude that at a level of 5%, there is a significant association between the occurrence of these features and the impression mark. As in all social science research, however, it is wise to interpret the results cautiously. Note that although the scripts had been marked by three different markers in order to ensure reliability and validity, one cannot necessarily be sure that the low marks are just due to the low quality of those scripts that achieved low marks. There is a possibility that the low marks might be due to the anti-Creole bias of the markers rather than to the quality of the writing in the scripts. The researchers themselves were satisfied that none of the markers held such views, but the issue might be investigated by giving the scripts to other markers for further assessment of impression mark. Validity is nearly always a problem for social science research. In this instance, the threat to the study's validity would come from the possibility that the impression marks were not a measure of the quality of the scripts but of the prejudices of the markers.

POSTSCRIPT

This chapter has summarized much of the whole book. It has involved the mathematical and statistical analysis of information, and it has shown how the use of a computer can perform all the routine calculations far more quickly and accurately than one could ever hope to do. Of course, it is still necessary to understand the basis for the mathematics and the statistics, otherwise one would never be sure that the computer was doing the right thing. One must also be able to interpret the results that have been obtained from the computer.

Many people who are very efficient in their own sphere of work or study think themselves incompetent when it comes to numerical work, and dread the day when they will have to spend many tedious hours in calculation. We hope that this book has shown that armed with a computer, the most number-fearing person can handle complicated calculations with efficiency and with confidence in the accuracy of the results.

Glossary of computer jargon

Address	Each item of a *spreadsheet* has an address to tell you where it is. The address G7, for example, refers to the cell in the G column and the 7 row.
Application	A program which performs a task. *Word-processors* and *spreadsheets* are examples of applications.
ASCII	American Standard Code for Information Exchange. A code which converts letters into numbers. All common *word-processors* use this code, so it can be used to transfer a document from one word-processor to another.
Backup	To make a copy of a file. This ensures that your work will not be lost if the original version is destroyed.
BIOS	Basic Input and Output System. The instructions which are activated when you switch on the computer. It enables the computer to receive and transmit information.
Bit	The basic building block of computer memory. It can register either 0 or 1.
Boot	To start the computer.
Bug	A mistake in a program which causes it to malfunction.
Byte	A byte is composed of 8 *bits*. A byte can register a number from 0 to 255. This number may code a single letter, for example.
Cache	A special area of memory which is used to hold data that have recently been used and might be used again.
CAD	Computer Aided Design. One of the uses of a computer.
CD ROM	A compact disk that can hold vast quantities of information. You can get data from it, but not write data on it. Hence ROM (Read Only Memory).
CGA	Colour Graphics Adaptor. A (comparatively) early device to send information from the computer to the screen.
Chip	A piece of silicon on which circuits of the computer are embedded.
Clone	A computer which will act like another is a clone of it. Any *PC* is a clone of the basic *IBM Personal Computer*.
Compatible	An item of either *hardware* or *software* which can be used in conjunction with other hardware or software is compatible with it.
CPU	Central Processing Unit. The core of a computer, which does all the calculations.
Database	An *application* which is used for handling large quantities of data.
Default	Suppose there is a choice to be made while using a computer. The default choice is the one the computer will make for you, unless you tell it otherwise.
Directory	A collection of *files*. The directories are linked together by a *tree*.
Disk	A device on which information can be recorded permanently.
DOS	Disk Operating System. The instructions which tell your computer what to do while you are using it.

Dot matrix	A printer, in which letters are formed by a pattern of tiny pins pressing onto the printer ribbon. There can be either 9 or 24 pins.
Drive	The device which holds a *disk*.
EGA	Enhanced Graphics Adaptor. More advanced than the *CGA*.
Field	Information in a *database* will be classified under various fields. If a database deals with customers, one of the fields will be their names.
File	Any collection of information which the computer can work on. *Programs*, documents you have written, lists of names are all examples of files.
Floppy	A floppy *disk* can be taken in and out of the computer.
Font	A particular size and shape of letters.
Format	To prepare a *disk* to be written on.
Gigabyte	A thousand (strictly 1024) *megabytes*.
GUI	Graphics User Interface. A way of instructing the computer by means of the *mouse* rather than by the keyboard.
Hard disk	A hard *disk* lives permanently inside the computer, and can hold much more information than a *floppy*.
Hardware	The solid machinery of the computer.
IBM	International Business Machines. The most important computer firm. In particular, it invented the *PC*.
Icon	A small picture which symbolizes a *program* or *file*. In a *WIMP* system you start the program or file by selecting the icon.
Inkjet	A printer which acts by squirting ink at the paper.
Kilobyte	A thousand (strictly 1024) *bytes*.
LAN	Local Area Network. A *network* linking computers in an office.
Laptop	A handbag-sized computer which can rest on your lap.
Laser	The most sophisticated form of printer.
LED	Light Emitting Diode. LED printers are almost as good as *lasers*. Often advertisements and salesmen blur the distinction between LED printers and lasers.
Macro	A collection of actions which can be performed with one single command.
Mainframe	A large computer, used by big institutions.
Megabyte	A million (strictly 1,048,576) *bytes*. 1 Megabyte equals 1024 *kilobytes*.
Memory	The circuits of a computer which hold the data and the programs while the computer is being used.
Menu	A list of the choices avaliable to you, from which you select one.
MHz	Megahertz. The speed of a computer is measured in MHz.
Micro	A small computer, such as a *PC*.
Mini	A middle-sized computer.
Modem	A device to connect a computer with the telephone system.
Mouse	A device, moved around the top of the table, to send instructions to the computer by moving a pointer around the screen.
Multitasking	Performing more than one task at the same time.
Network	The linking together of a group of computers, so that they can pass information to each other.
Operating system	The programs which control the basic operation of the computer.
Path	The route through the *directories* which leads to the *file* you want to use.
Personal Computer (PC)	A *micro*computer for individual use. In particular, those made by *IBM* and their *clones*.

Program	A sequence of instructions which tell the computer what to do.
Public domain	*Software* which can be used and copied without any copyright permission.
RAM	Random Access Memory. The memory of a computer, which you can write to as well as read from.
Record	An item in a *database*. A database of customers, for example, will have a record for each customer.
Relational database	A *database* which consists of many files linked together.
ROM	Read Only Memory. Computer memory which can be read from but not written to.
Shareware	*Software* which you can try out before you buy.
Software	The instructions and data which the *hardware* of a computer acts on.
Spreadsheet	An *application*, consisting of a grid of cells in which calculations can be done.
SVGA	Super *VGA*. Unlike *CGA*, *EGA* and *VGA*, this was not invented by *IBM*.
Systems files	The programs which control the basic operations of the computer.
Template	A pre-set form for documents.
Tracker-ball	A device like a *mouse*. It stays fixed, and you move a ball to control a pointer on the screen.
Tree	The structure of the files on a *disk*, showing how the *directories* lead on from each other.
VGA	Video Graphics Array. One stage on from *EGA*.
Virus	A *program* which attaches itself to other programs, and harms the working of the computer.
WIMP	Windows Icons Menus Pointer. A *GUI* way of controlling the computer.
Windows	A *multitasking* system, in which all the tasks you are using are displayed in 'windows' on the screen.
WYSIWYG	What You See Is What You Get. When the display on the screen is what you will get printed out on paper.

Answers to exercises

Chapter 1

Page 8	(a) £2,800,989	(b) 85,000	(c) £1,112,000 and £14,456,000
	(d) 57,000 and £855,000	(e) £12,000	(f) 19,000,000 ecus
	(g) £136		
Page 10	(a) $\frac{2}{5}$	(b) $\frac{3}{50}$	(c) $\frac{11}{15}$
	(d) $\frac{1}{15}$		
Page 11	(a) 250	(b) $\frac{49}{250}$	(c) $\frac{1}{75}$
Page 13	(a) 500 and 2.5%	(b) 200 and $3\frac{1}{3}$%	(c) 600,000 and 1,000,000
Page 14	(a) £700,000	(b) 3000	(c) 17,268,750
Page 14	(a) 80,000	(b) 728	(c) 20,000 and 15,000
Page 15	(a) 2000	(b) 30,000	
Page 16	(a) −20, 10 and 30	(b) −£10,000	
Page 18	(a) £10,711	(b) £3201	(c) £1,651,647
	(d) 5 and 9	(e) 3804: 6956 and 2845: 959	(f) 3%
	(g) 62:325	(h) 4:13	(i) £78,778 and 12; 21
	(j) 65:387		

Chapter 2

Page 21	(a) 200	(b) $230	(c) £21,500
Page 23	(a) 240 ml	(b) £512,000	(c) 8:15
	(d) 284,125 and 204,911; 489,036; 5,379,396	(e) 70 and 14; 140	(f) £6.90; £72.0; £105
Page 25	(a) 30,700,000 and £370,000,000.	(b) 110 and 7	
Page 25	(a) 1.0% and 9.13%	(b) 63 and 55	(c) 520
Page 27	(a) 36,800,000	(b) 0.19, 0.12, 0.70	(c) DM3100
	(d) 1.66		
Page 29	(a) 144 square feet and 1728 cu. feet	(b) 529 and 13	
Page 30	*Statistical formulas*: mean 88, variance 42.8.		
Page 30	(a) £8590	(b) 8.4%	(c) £14
	(d) £1906	(e) £40	(f) £100

Chapter 3

Page 35	(a) $456	(b) 2.4 ml	(c) 0.75
	(d) 14,000	(e) 40,536,000	
Page 36	(a) 8,5P	(b) 100m/a	(c) $MV = PQ$

	(d) $I - E$ and $0.2(I - E)$		
Page 42	(a) 6	(b) 2	
Page 43	(a) $x = (m - 5)/3$	(b) $x = (30 - C)/5$	(c) $V = PQ/M$
	(d) $m = ax/100$; $a = 100m/x$	(e) $c = 2b - a$	(f) $(AS - T)/(A - 1)$
Page 45	(a) $\bar{x} = 4.5$; $\bar{y} = 1.975$; var$(x) = 5.25$; var$(y) = 0.574375$; $r = 0.972$		
Page 46	(a) 78.5	(b) yes	(c) 4

Chapter 4

Page 56	(a) nominal	(b) ordinal	(c) numerical
	(d) numerical	(e) numerical	(f) nominal
Page 58	(a) ordinal	(b) semi-skilled working class	(c) skilled working class
	(d) no		
Page 59	(a) 16	(b) 13.86 years	
Page 60	(a) 3 and 3	(b) 0.015 and 0.00275	(c) 0.00025 and 0.0000095
Page 63	(a) 0.463	(b) 0.914	
Page 65	(a) $C = 0.980P - 8.52$	(b) 35.6%	

Chapter 6

Page 84	(a) $z = 1.79$ sig. (one-tailed test)	(b) $z = 1.12$. non-sig.	
Page 87	(a) $r = -0.974$. sig.	(b) r = 0.897. sig.	(c) $r = -0.9959$. sig
Page 89	(a) $z = 2.79$. sig.	(b) $z = 2.12$. sig	
Page 91	(a) $z = 1.74$. sig. (one-tailed test)	(b) $z = 1.55$ not sig.	
Page 94	(a) $\chi^2(3) = 35$ sig.	(b) $\chi^2(2) = 12.46$ sig.	(c) $\chi^2(6) = 27.4$ sig.
Page 97	(a) 49.8 to 54.2	(b) 28.6 to 31.4	

Index